GW01458862

THE PRAYER LIFE OF
JESUS

*Developing yours
by looking at His*

GLENN AREKION

Copyright © 2018 Glenn Arekion

All rights reserved under the international copyright law. No part of this book may be reproduced or transmitted in any form or by any means, electronic or mechanical, including photocopying, recording, or by any information storage and retrieval system, without the express, written permission of the author or the publisher. The exception is reviewers, who may quote brief passages in a review.

Faith House Publishing

ISBN 978-1-943282-10-4

faithhousepublishing.com

Unless otherwise marked, all Scripture quotations are taken from the King James Version of the Bible.

Scripture quotations marked (NLT) are taken from the Holy Bible, New Living Translation, copyright © 1996, 2004, 2007 by Tyndale House Foundation. Used by permission of Tyndale House Publishers, Inc., Carol Stream, Illinois 60188. All rights reserved.

Scripture quotations marked (JUB) are taken from The Jubilee Bible, copyright © 2000, 2001, 2010 by Life Sentence Publishing, Aneko Press, from the Scriptures of the Reformation, edited by Russell M. Stendal. All rights reserved. Used by permission.

Scripture quotations marked (TLB) are taken from The Living Bible, copyright © 1971. Used by permission of Tyndale House Publishers, Inc., Carol Stream, Illinois 60188. All rights reserved.

Scripture quotations marked (NASB) are taken from the New American Standard Bible®, copyright © 1960, 1962, 1963, 1968, 1971, 1972, 1973, 1975, 1977, 1995 by The Lockman Foundation. Used by permission of Lockman.org.

Scripture quotations marked (AMP) are taken from the Amplified® Bible, copyright © 1954, 1958, 1962, 1964, 1965, 1987 by The Lockman Foundation. Used by permission of Lockman.org.

Scripture quotations marked (NIV) are taken from The Holy Bible, New International Version®, NIV®, copyright © 1973, 1978, 1984, 2011 by Biblica, Inc.™ Used by permission. All rights reserved worldwide.

Scripture quotations marked (WNT) are taken from The Weymouth New Testament, also known as The New Testament in Modern Speech or The Modern Speech New Testament. A translation from the text of The Resultant Greek Testament by Richard Francis Weymouth first published in 1903. In the public domain.

Scripture quotations marked (ISV) are taken from the Holy Bible: International Standard Version®. Copyright © 1996–forever by The ISV Foundation. All rights reserved internationally. Used by permission.

Scripture quotations marked (ARAM) are taken from The Original Aramaic New Testament in Plain English. Translated by Rev. Glenn David Bauscher. Copyright © 2012 Glenn David Bauscher. Used by permission.

Scripture quotations marked (NET Bible) are from the NET Bible®, copyright © 1996-2006 by Biblical Studies Press, L.L.C. Netbible.com. All rights reserved. Used by permission.

Scripture quotations marked (NCV) are from the New Century Version®, copyright © 2005 by Thomas Nelson, Inc. Used by permission. All rights reserved.

Further definitions taken from The NIV Theological Dictionary of New Testament Words (Zondervan Publishing House), W. E Vine's Expository Of New Testament Words, Adam's Clarke Commentary, Pulpit's Commentary.

Printed in the United States of America

CONTENTS

INTRODUCTION

J ESUS said, '*My house shall be called the house of prayer*'. It is the divine call of every believer to be a person of prayer because through it we:

- ❖ Draw near to God.
- ❖ Appropriate miracles.
- ❖ Put a stop to the attacks of the devil.
- ❖ Invoke divine intervention.
- ❖ Give birth to prophetic destinies.

Sadly today the church is filled with people who have no prayer life and consequently are wide open to the destructive arrows of the wicked one. The strength of a believer is determined by the Word abiding in him and him abiding in the presence of God in prayer. It is my joy to bring you this treatise on prayer as we look extensively at the prayer life of our Lord and Savior Jesus Christ. It is my hope that you will have a desire to pray with our Master for this is His present day ministry. In this book we will look at how Jesus prayed and the different depths and dimensions of prayer that He taught us. Once you are acquainted with them then you can use them as weapons to wield against the enemy to stop him and to bring you your desired results.

You will be excited to pray when you get results. Prayer is not meant to be a boring chore. The only reason you think prayer is boring is because you do not know much about it. It is my prayer that you will discover the great feats that can be achieved through prayer. Let this be your cry today, 'Lord, teach me to pray!'

I was struck by what A.W Tozer wrote many years ago:

'What profit is there in prayer? Much every way. Whatever God can do faith can do, and whatever faith can do prayer can do when it is offered in faith. An invitation to prayer is, therefore, an invitation to omnipotence, for prayer engages the Omnipotent God and brings Him into our human affairs. Nothing is impossible to the man who prays in faith, just as nothing is impossible with God. This generation has yet to prove all that prayer can do for believing men and women.'

This, my friend needs to be the reality in your life! As you leaf through the pages of this book, it is my prayer that you will catch the spirit of prayer, making the impossible bow before you as it did before the Lord Jesus. Who else is better qualified to teach you about prayer than Jesus Himself?

Let Jesus be your teacher and prayer partner today!

LORD, TEACH ME TO PRAY

CHAPTER 1
LORD, TEACH ME TO PRAY

And it came to pass, that, as he was praying in a certain place, when he ceased, one of his disciples said unto him, Lord, teach us to pray, as John also taught his disciples.

LUKE 11:1

Jesus, our Lord and Redeemer was a man of prayer while He was on the earth and right now in heaven His present day ministry is one of prayer and intercession. Both aspects of His life on earth and in heaven was and is saturated with prayer. He had a strong prayer life as did many in the Old and New Testament. The strength of your life is determined by the abiding presence of the Word in you and your abiding presence before God in prayer.

Today, one of the greatest flaws in the lives of millions of believers is the weakness of their prayer lives. We have heard about others who obtained great miracles through the potency of prayer. We know if we apply the same diligence we would also procure the same divine providence and yet our negligence or coldness in prayer persists causing much wretchedness. As the old idiom goes, *Prayerless Christianity is powerless Christianity*.

We simply cannot live the Christian life successfully without prayer. Through it we commune with the God of heaven and we appropriate our needs and desires. It is through prayer that we intercede for others and it is through prayer that the opposing forces of darkness are bound. We will see this in the life of our Lord Jesus.

The strength of your life is determined by the abiding presence of the Word in you and your abiding presence before God in prayer

One day, after Jesus finished His praying, one of His disciples (who clearly felt the impact) asked Jesus to teach them to pray. In effect he was asking him, 'How do I develop my prayer life?' He observed the prayer life of Jesus and desired to have the same. Many times we misunderstand this verse and think it says, 'Lord, teach us *how* to pray' but clearly it says, 'Lord, teach us to pray'. What's the difference you may ask? Many of us know how to pray; we know the principles and different types of prayer. We even know the different rules of engagement in prayer but our problem is that we simply do not pray. We do not give prayer the stretch of time and the place of priority it deserves in our lives. This is very important when it comes to developing your prayer life. To develop a strong prayer life, the believer must understand the priority, the place and the period of time given to prayer determines its potency. It is through praying that we learn to pray.

There is a notion in the modern church that to give little time to prayer is sufficient because God understands our hectic lives. This is foolish and has produced many powerless and fruitless believers. No one has ever been more busy than the Lord Jesus; no one in existence ever had the demands made upon their life like the Lord. We read that Jesus' life was so hectic He did not even have time to eat:

> *And the multitude cometh together again, so that they could not so much as eat bread. And when his friends heard of it, they went out to lay hold on him: for they said, He is beside himself.*
>
> MARK 3:20-21

While Jesus did not make time to eat He definitely made time to pray. The demanding crowd stopped Him from eating but did not stop Him from the place of praying. This clearly shows his priority:

> *But so much the more went there a fame abroad of him: and great multitudes came together to hear, and to be healed by him of their infirmities. **And he withdrew himself into the wilderness, and prayed.***
>
> LUKE 5:15-16

He never allowed the fruitfulness of ministry to hamper His prayer life because He knew the only reason there was power in public ministry was due to the power of personal ministering to God. The mistake many of us have made is that we obtain things in prayer which are subsequently lost due to prayerlessness that follows. There is just no way around it: time and priority must be given to prayer. Ample time given to prayer will amplify your life. The reason we are not able to give ample time to prayer is because we have not been *taught* to give time to prayer. Jesus astonishingly asked His disciples when He found them asleep on prayer duty, '*What, could ye not watch with me one hour?*' (Matthew 26:40).

To develop a strong prayer life, the believer must understand the priority, the place and the period of time given to prayer determines its potency

Many have frustratingly gone through this ordeal and I am sure you are also a candidate: you started praying and you prayed up a storm then thought to yourself, 'surely I've been praying for nearly an hour!', only to look at your watch to see it's been just twelve minutes! Then the pain hits you: the fact there are still forty eight minutes left. Many – including ministers and pastors – struggle to pray for a whole hour, just like the disciples who could not keep up with Jesus in the Garden of Gethsemane. Yet in the garden, Jesus prayed for *three* hours because when Jesus said, 'Could you not watch with me', it referred to a three hour segment. A *watch* in the Scriptures refers to a three hour segment. In other words 12am– 3am is a watch, 3am–6am is a watch and this applies to every three hour segment after. It is interesting to see that the Bible records that Jesus prayed for one hour, three hours, nine hours and all night before God. The Bible is also full of men and women of prayer who had power with God and power with men. They had power over the heavens and power over the earth.

❦ Men and women of prayer

* Abraham, the father of faith was a great praying man and an intercessor.
* Jacob was the prince of prevailing prayer.
* Moses held such authority in prayer that he could change the mind of God and his intercessory prayers had direct implications in battles.
* Elijah closed and opened the heavens by his prayers.
* Hannah broke barrenness through her consistent prayers.
* Esther was a mighty warrior in prayer and saved the Jews from total annihilation.
* Daniel prayed Israel out of the Babylonian captivity.
* Jonah prayed his way out of the whale.
* Anna, the prophetess prayed through the coming of the Messiah.
* John the Baptist imparted his strong life of prayer into his disciples.
* Jesus, our great high priest is right now interceding for us at the right hand of the Father.
* Peter and John were prayer warriors.
* James, the brother of Jesus was nicknamed 'Camel knees' due to his prayer life.
* The early church was given and devoted to prayer.
* Paul was a great prayer champion.

Prayer is not an invention of preachers to drag people to church. Prayer started at the beginning in Genesis:

And Adam knew his wife again; and she bare a son, and called his name Seth: For God, said she, hath appointed me another seed instead of Abel, whom Cain slew. And to Seth, to him also there was born a son; and he called his name Enos: then began men to call upon the name of the Lord.
GENESIS 4:25-26

After Cain killed Abel, Eve gave birth to Seth who later had a son whom Adam named Enos. Albert Barnes' Commentary on this verse is enlightening:

A son is born to Sheth also, whom he calls Enosh. In this name there is probably an allusion to the meaning of sickliness and dependence which belongs to the root word. These qualities were now found to be characteristic of man in his present state.

We pray because we are dependent upon God. We pray because in ourselves we are frail but when we pray we tap into the omnipotence of the Almighty. As the great British stalwart preacher Charles Spurgeon said a long time ago, *'Prayer is the slender nerve that moves the muscle of omnipotence.'* Anybody who has ever done anything of significance in the world for the kingdom of God has been a person of prayer. You too can be a champion in prayer. Jesus quoted from Isaiah and they both revealed God's eternal commission for his people:

For My house shall be called a house of prayer for all nations.
ISAIAH 56:7

And He said to them, "It is written, 'My house shall be called a house of prayer...
MATTHEW. 21:13

The word 'house' in Greek is *oikos* meaning *family*. In essence Jesus was saying 'my family is called to be a family of prayer.' You and I form part of the constitution of the family of God. We have been called to pray. Every believer – without exception – has been called to a life of prayer, from new believers to the seasoned old saints. You will see great and supernatural change in your life as you embark on this developing journey.

Prayer is not learned in a classroom but in the closet – E.M Bounds

Your prayer life needs no longer to be a source of frustration for you. As you see results it will amplify your prayer life even more. As you experience more breakthroughs and break out moments through your prayers, you will seek to be in the place of prayer. You will have deep experiences, great adventures and continuous intimacy with God as you continue to pray. There is no mystery to a great prayer life. It is through praying that we learn how to pray. It is through praying that we develop a strong and vibrant prayer life. I love this quote from Martin Luther: '*No one can believe how powerful prayer is and what it can effect except those who have learnt it by experience.*'

This quote so fitly describes our predicament; it is through praying that our prayer life will be developed. Some have said that they don't have a strong prayer life because they don't have the ministry of an intercessor. You will notice that Paul does not mention intercession as part of the office of the fivefold ministry: apostle, prophet, evangelist, pastor and teacher. (Ephesians 4:11). Why? Because not everyone is called to the fivefold ministry offices but **every believer is called to intercede.** In other words every believer is called to the ministry of intercession, which is prayer. When we pray and intercede we are partnering with the present day ministry of the Lord Jesus:

*Who is he that condemneth? It is Christ that died, yea rather, that is risen again, who is even at the right hand of God, **who also maketh intercession for us.***
ROMANS 8:34

*Wherefore he is able also to save them to the uttermost that come unto God by him, **seeing he ever liveth to make intercession for them.***
HEBREWS 7:25

*There is no mystery to a great prayer life.
It is through praying that we learn how to pray*

Jesus is presently at the right hand of God in prayer and intercession. This is his present day ministry. Bear in mind that Jesus told us that God is looking for a certain type of person. In the Gospel of John He told us that God is looking for true worshipers that will worship in spirit and in truth (John 4:23). Secondly we are told:

Ye have not gone up into the gaps, neither made up the hedge for the house of Israel to stand in the battle in the day of the Lord.

EZEKIEL 13:5

The people of the land have used oppression, and exercised robbery, and have vexed the poor and needy: yea, they have oppressed the stranger wrongfully. ***And I sought for a man among them, that should make up the hedge, and stand in the gap*** *before me for the land, that I should not destroy it: but I found none.*

EZEKIEL 22:29-30

God is looking for those who will stand in the gap and Solomon informed us that if the hedge is broken then a serpent or the devil will bite him (Ecclesiastes 10:8). There is a dire need for men and women of prayer today. God is looking for such who will stand in the gap and change the destinies of churches, cities and nations. Are you one that will respond to the call of prayer? Are you ready to be taught to delve into the depths and dimensions of prayer? I believe you are! The future belongs to those who pray. As you go through the pages of this book, your heart will be stirred to pray as you discover the in-workings and practical outworking of prayer.

No one can believe how powerful prayer is and what it can effect except those who have learnt it by experience – Martin Luther

In this book, it is my desire to drive you forward in your prayer life. The spirit of faith is the spirit of prayer and when we operate in strong faith we will have a strong prayer life: faith is released by prayer and prayer is an expression of our faith. Both Abraham and Jesus – who were men with strong faith – were given to prayer. So if you consider yourself to be a person of strong faith then you will have a strong prayer life.

Here are three things that happen when you fail to pray:

1. You will faint

And he spake a parable unto them to this end, that men ought always to pray, and not to faint;

LUKE 18:1

2. Your faith will fail

But I have prayed for thee, that thy faith fail not: and when thou art converted, strengthen thy brethren.

LUKE 22:32

3. You will fall

Watch and pray so that you will not fall into temptation. The spirit is willing, but the flesh is weak.

MATTHEW 26:41

Let us rise in prayer in order to fulfill our destiny. Let us look at the prayer life of Jesus in order to develop ours. We can get no greater example than the Lord himself.

To be a Christian without prayer is no more possible than to be alive without breathing

CHAPTER 2
THE PRAYER LIFE OF JESUS – PART ONE

*"Who **in the days of his flesh, when he had offered up prayers and supplications with strong crying** and tears unto him that was able to save him from death, and was heard in that he feared;"*
HEBREWS 5:7

While Jesus lived on earth, he prayed to God and asked God for help. He prayed with loud cries and tears to the One who could save him from death, and his prayer was heard because he trusted God.
NEW CENTURY VERSION

In the days of His flesh, Jesus offered up much prayers. He was a man of prayer. The synoptic Gospels are not just a biography of Jesus' life and ministry, they also give us an insight into His prayer life. People will buy biographies to read and glean from the lives of successful people. Whether it is about Steve Jobs or Bill Gates, people endeavor to read in order to extract any secrets to implement in their own lives. The synoptic Gospels unveil the secrets to the earthly ministry of Jesus, while the epistles and the book of Revelation unveil the secrets of His heavenly ministry. In His earthly ministry you will notice that between all the major events and miracles in His life, there was a saturation of prayer. Although He was the Son of God He operated on the earth as a man anointed with the Holy Spirit. In everything that He did He leaned upon the Spirit of God; this is why He had a strong prayer life. Prayer gave Jesus authority, power and access into the realm of the miraculous, empowering Him over the natural, causing it to bow before the mighty power of God.

We can look at the life and earthly ministry of Jesus this way:

❖ Prayer – Miracles – Prayer
❖ Prayer – Major Events – Prayer

Since Jesus' life was saturated with prayer, who else is better qualified to teach us prayer than the Lord himself? He is the author and the finisher of our faith. We can develop our prayer life to be strong and effective by looking at the strong prayer life of Jesus. His earthly walk is to be reflected in our earthly walk. Let us look at His prayer life and extract powerful secrets to implement in our lives. I will endeavor to mark your thinking by making all the points begin with the letter P.

The synoptic Gospels unveil the secrets to the earthly ministry of Jesus while the epistles and the book of Revelation unveil the secrets of His heavenly ministry.

Jesus made prayer His PRIORITY

He protected His prayer life:

But so much the more went there a fame abroad of him: and great multitudes came together to hear, and to be healed by him of their infirmities. And he withdrew himself into the wilderness, and prayed.
LUKE 5:15-16

When life and ministry's demands pressed upon Him to the point of being unusually busy, Jesus withdrew to a private place to pray. He protected His prayer life from the general busyness of life. Unfortunately we make excuses for our prayerlessness with the busyness of our lives; we claim that we are so busy we can find no time to pray. On the other hand, the more intense and busy Jesus' life became, the more He prayed and the more He protected His prayer life – at all cost, giving it utmost priority. If you do not make the deliberate act of protecting your prayer life, it is just a matter of time before it will be on the back burner. At one point Jesus was so busy that He had no time to eat and his friends and family thought he was crazy:

> *And the multitude cometh together again, so that they could not so much as eat bread. And when his friends heard of it, they went out to lay hold on him: for they said, He is beside himself.*
>
> MARK 3:20-21

Look at the sequence that Mark portrayed of the busyness and demands made upon Jesus and yet how he zealously guarded His prayer life:

> *And he said unto them, Come ye yourselves apart into a desert place, and rest a while: **for there were many coming and going, and they had no leisure so much as to eat.** And they departed into a desert place by ship privately. And the people saw them departing, and many knew him, and ran afoot thither out of all cities, and outwent them, and came together unto him. And Jesus, when he came out, saw much people, and was moved with compassion toward them, because they were as sheep not having a shepherd: and he began to teach them many things....And straightway he constrained his disciples to get into the ship, and to go to the other side before unto Bethsaida, while he sent away the people. **And when he had sent them away, he departed into a mountain to pray.***
>
> MARK 6:31-34, 45-46

Jesus took the initiative in prayer; He did not allow the ministry, family or life to crowd out His prayer life. Even when He and the disciples found time and place to rest, He went alone to God in prayer. He sent His close disciples – his co-workers – away, in order to spend time in the presence of His Father. He pressed in prayer and this is a great secret for the success of the ministry of Jesus. *Ministering to God* is our *first* ministry before we can ever effectively minister to people. Great men have lost their cutting edge because they did not learn this secret and allowed *ministry to people* to substitute for *ministry to God* in prayer. **You will not have a ministry of power to the people if you do not have a ministry of prayer to God.**

> ## My question to you is, Are you protecting your prayer life and keeping it your utmost priority?

I have so much to do that I shall spend the first three hours in prayer – Martin Luther

ৎ Jesus made prayer his DAILY PRACTICE

*And He came out and went, **as was His habit**, to the Mount of Olives, and the disciples also followed Him. And when He came to the place, He said to them, Pray that you may not [at all] enter into temptation.*

LUKE 22:39-40
AMPLIFIED BIBLE

*And Aaron shall burn thereon sweet incense **every morning**: when he dresseth the lamps, he shall burn incense upon it. And when Aaron lighteth the lamps at even, **he shall burn incense upon it, a perpetual incense before the Lord throughout your generations.***

EXODUS 30:7-8

Every morning when Aaron maintains the lamps, he must burn fragrant incense on the altar...

EXODUS 30:8
NEW LIVING TRANSLATION

And every priest standeth daily ministering...

HEBREWS 10:11

The priest in the Old Testament was to burn incense daily to God in the morning and evening. The comparison of prayer with incense is in accordance with Old Testament language, with incense being the emblem of prayer as David unveiled: '*Let my prayer be set forth before thee as incense; and the lifting up of my hands as the evening sacrifice*' (Psalm 141:2).

This is also illustrated in the book of Revelation:

*And when He had taken the scroll, the four living creatures and the twenty-four elders fell down before the Lamb, each having a harp, and golden bowls being **full of incenses, which are the prayers of the saints.***

REVELATION 5:8
BEREA LITERAL BIBLE

*And another angel came and stood at the altar, having a golden censer; and there was given unto him much **incense, that he should offer it with the prayers of all saints** upon the golden altar which was before the throne. **And the smoke of the incense, which came with the prayers of the saints, ascended up before God** out of the angel's hand.*

REVELATION 8:3-4

As a praying priest, Jesus would pray daily to His Father. It was His habit to pray daily. **Your habit determines your destiny.** It is not what you do once in a while that will impact your life but *what you do daily*. Steve Jobs talked about one daily habit that made the biggest impact on his life and work. Habit triggers the law of eventuality. In other words if you keep doing something over and over again, eventually something is going to happen. For example, if a person keeps smoking forty cigarettes daily, eventually his lungs will be damaged with cancer. There's no rocket science behind this, it's just a fact. Habits work for you when they are good and they work against you when they are bad. Jesus also told us to pray: '*Give us this day our daily bread*'. It is your daily prayer that will bring daily benefits.

Blessed be the Lord, who daily loadeth us with benefits, even the God of our salvation. Selah.

PSALM 68:19

Jesus prayed ceaselessly and incessantly to God. He was continuously in prayer mode. The Psalmist declared, '*Be merciful unto me, O Lord: for I cry unto thee daily*' (Psalm 86:3). Again we see another declaration,

'*...Lord, I have called daily upon thee, **I have stretched out my hands unto thee**'* (Psalm 88:9). Here is another portion in Psalms revealing daily prayer:

> *As for me, I will call upon God; and the Lord shall save me. **Evening, and morning, and at noon**, will I pray, and cry aloud: and he shall hear my voice.*
>
> PSALM 55:16-17

It is in your daily prayer that you develop a strong prayer life. So many times I hear people ask, '*How do I develop my prayer life?*' It is through praying that you develop your prayer life. This is why daily prayer is important: it stretches your capacity in prayer. Daily praying enables you to lean on the Lord and it also trains you to effectively wield the weapon of prayer. As soldiers and Marines undergo rigorous training – embedding the knowledge of their weapons in their psyche so when they encounter a sudden combat situation they instinctively know how to handle them – the same thing occurs in you as you pray daily: training you to use prayer as a weapon of war when under pressure or facing spiritual warfare.

It is through praying that you develop your prayer life

§ Jesus had a SPECIAL PLACE for prayer

> *And in the morning, rising up a great while before day, he went out, and departed into a solitary place, and there prayed.*
>
> MARK 1:35

Jesus had a specific place for prayer. Notice it was a solitary place; a place of no distraction. This is a major key to developing a strong prayer life. It was a place that was set apart and separated from noise and distraction. We are by far the most distracted generation that has ever existed, with all the latest gadgets and technology. We need to make a place where we are separated from all these distractions.

I want you to see the testimony of the four Gospel writers:

*And when he had sent the multitudes away, **he went up into a mountain
apart to pray:** and when the evening was come, he was there alone.*
MATTHEW 14:23

*And when he had sent them away, **he departed into a mountain to pray.***
MARK 6:46

*And it came to pass in those days, that **he went out into a mountain to
pray,** and continued all night in prayer to God.*
LUKE 6:12

*When Jesus therefore perceived that they would come and take him by
force, to make him a king, **he departed again into a mountain himself
alone.***
JOHN 6:15

All four Gospel authors categorically specified that Jesus went up the
mountain to pray, with Dr Luke further expounding: '*And He came out
and went, **as was His habit,** to the Mount of Olives...*' (Luke 22:39 Amplified
Bible). It was Jesus' habit to go on the mountain to pray! We know that we
can pray everywhere and anywhere but any serious student of prayer will
know that a specific place of prayer becomes an altar where one meets with
God. This place becomes a special place of divine encounter that, like Jacob,
we can call it Peniel, meaning '*I have seen God face to face*' (Genesis 32:30).
Daniel also had a specific place of prayer: '*Now when Daniel knew that the
writing was signed, he went into his house; and his windows being open in his
chamber toward Jerusalem, he kneeled upon his knees three times a day, and
prayed, and gave thanks before his God, **as he did aforetime**'* (Daniel 6:10).

Choose for yourself a place; make it your special place of encounter with
God. I have been to John Wesley's house in London and have seen his prayer
closet, his place of encounter with God. No wonder he impacted England and
America. Do you have a place where you meet with God on a continuous basis?

For me, I have a room in my house where nothing happens *except* prayer. I call it my Holy Room, a Secret Place for divine encounter. Most of my praying and book writing is done in that room when I am home. There is nothing there to distract me; there are only two comfortable sofas, a side table with a lampshade and an ottoman.

O, let the place of secret prayer become to me the most beloved spot on earth – Andrew Murray

---

You may not have a holy room but you can have a chair or a place in your house where it is just you and God. It could be your office. I heard of someone who would lock himself in his office at lunch time and bow before God under his desk to pray and seek God. Some people go on a prayer walk. How about you? I also do a prayer walk. That is another weapon in my repertoire for a strong prayer life. I live in a quiet neighborhood so there's no heavy traffic disturbing my prayer. Choose a specific place in your home and dedicate it to your time with the Lord. When you create a secret place where you just pray, as time goes by you will notice your desire to be in that particular place grows. The more you use it and keep that room for prayer or spiritual things only, your prayer room will become a holy and sanctified place, a glory room where God meets with you. As I have said before, you can pray anywhere but if you want to develop a strong prayer life, you need to learn the secret of making a special place for you and God.

> **My question to you is, Do you have a special place that you have set apart to meet with your God?**

ॐ **Jesus advocated PRIVACY in prayer.**

*And when he had sent the multitudes away, **he went up into a mountain apart to pray**: and when the evening was come, **he was there alone.***
MATTHEW 14:23

*And when he had sent them away, he departed into a **mountain to pray**.*

MARK 6:46

*And it came to pass in those days, that he went out into a **mountain to pray**, and continued all night in prayer to God.*

LUKE 6:12

*When Jesus therefore perceived that they would come and take him by force, to make him a king, he departed again into **a mountain himself alone**.*

JOHN 6:15

As great as *corporate prayer* is (and there is a need for it), we see that Jesus spent time alone in God's presence. I really like how Mark pens Jesus' prayer life:

And in the morning, rising up a great while before day, he went out, and departed into a solitary place, and there prayed.

MARK 1:35

Jesus deliberately moved away from the crowd. A crowd indicates noise, hustling and bustling, clamoring for your attention. He deliberately moved to a solitary place. Jesus knew it was not possible to connect with the Father surrounded by so much noise, commotion and pandemonium baying for His attention. He knew that the secret to a strong prayer life was privacy; Jesus wanted undisturbed fellowship with God. You will notice that Jesus prayed through the night or very early in the morning because he wanted to be completely absorbed in God's presence and not be distracted by the noise of the world. It is in the privacy of prayer that we develop intimacy with God. Then, intimacy triggers accuracy in the Spirit. You see, there are many distractions without and within that we must deal with.

Privacy - Intimacy - Accuracy

The private devotion of Jesus to the Father resulted in the public display of the manifestations of the Holy Spirit in His life and ministry. When He taught on prayer, Jesus emphasized privacy: *'But thou, when thou prayest, enter into thy closet, and when thou hast **shut thy door**, pray to thy Father which is in secret; and thy Father which seeth in secret shall reward thee openly'* (Matthew 6:6). What is the point of shutting the door? It is the shutting out of distractions. Isn't it amazing that the moment you begin to pray, your sense of hearing becomes so acute that you can hear every single noise? You can hear the clock ticking, the mosquito and fly buzzing and the sound of your breathing. Any kind of noise can trigger a loss of concentration during your time of prayer. Jesus was well aware of our plight and this is why He emphasized privacy.

The practical reasons for privacy are important, but there is also a more subtle reason in Jesus' advice to pray in secret. You must understand this: God will not compete for your attention. He will not compete with anything or anyone for an audience with you. God wants exclusivity. He clearly said in his Word, *'Thou shalt have no other gods before me'* (Exodus 20:3). You cannot be enamored with somebody if you have an attitude of all-inclusive relationships. It is through *exclusivity* that the other party feels special and sought out. It is through privacy of prayer that you will discover the Fatherhood of God, the High Priesthood of Jesus and the Comfort of the Holy Spirit. Simply put, it is in the privacy of prayer that you will know the person of God and the plans of God.

> *And after six days Jesus taketh Peter, James, and John his brother, and bringeth them up into an high mountain **apart**, And was **transfigured before them**: and his face did shine as the sun, and his raiment was white as the light. And, behold, there appeared unto them Moses and Elias talking with him.*
>
> MATTHEW 17:1-3

> *And, behold, there talked with him two men, which were Moses and Elias: Who appeared in glory, and spake of his decease which he should*

*accomplish at Jerusalem. But Peter and they that were with him were heavy with sleep: and **when they were awake, they saw his glory**, and the two men that stood with him. And it came to pass, as they departed from him, Peter said unto Jesus, Master, it is good for us to be here: and let us make three tabernacles; one for thee, and one for Moses, and one for Elias: not knowing what he said. While he thus spake, **there came a cloud**, and overshadowed them: and they feared as they **entered into the cloud**. And there came a voice out of the cloud, saying, This is my beloved Son: hear him. And when the voice was past, Jesus was found alone.*

LUKE 9:30-36

God will not compete with anything or anyone for an audience with you. God wants exclusivity

Notice that this special private prayer meeting was with three handpicked disciples, Peter, James and John, who would be the future pillars of the early church. He took them apart and there, Jesus was transfigured before them and they saw His glory, they saw Moses and Elijah, they entered a cloud and heard the audible voice of God. Notice these four things happened in prayer. What are the significances?

1 Jesus was transfigured before them and they saw His glory

In the privacy of prayer they saw the glory of Jesus. It is when we go to God privately in prayer that Jesus will become more than just a great historical figure recorded on the pages of an old book. You will see Him in His glory; you will experience Him as your High Priest, your Advocate, your Healer and Redeemer.

It is through privacy of prayer that you will discover the Fatherhood of God, the High Priesthood of Jesus and the Comfort of the Holy Spirit

2 They saw Moses and Elijah

The significance of the appearance of Moses and Elijah is not only that they were major past prophets of the Old Testament that showed up in a different era effecting lives but that they are symbolic of the Scriptures. Moses represented the Law and Elijah the Prophets. The Old testament was made up of the Law and the Prophets. In other words, it is through the privacy of prayer that the Scriptures came alive to them. Something and someone who lived so long ago became real to them.

3 They entered a cloud

The cloud is symbolic of the Holy Spirit and the glory of God. In the privacy of prayer, the Glory cloud overshadowed them, in the same way the Holy Spirit came upon Mary to bring into the earth the Incarnate one. When the Holy Spirit comes upon and overshadows you, the glory will descend upon you and you will bring great things upon the earth.

4 They heard the voice of God.

In the privacy of prayer, intimacy is born which will make you sensitive to His voice. They heard the audible voice of God and if God so chooses, you may hear His audible voice. However many times because of the accuracy that is borne through intimacy, the still small voice of God in your spirit man sounds just as if God spoke to you in an audible voice. I like to call it *tapping into the inaudible voice of God*. This is done in your spirit man. Private prayer prepares your heart to tap into the promptings of the Spirit.

*Private prayer prepares your heart
to tap into the promptings of the Spirit*

ᕫ Jesus gave prayer PROTRACTED PERIOD

Time invested in prayer will always result in power and productivity. The time element in prayer is of huge importance. Jesus invested a lot of time in prayer. Today we want to pray short prayers and see great and quick manifestations. Many pray short prayers and don't see any results. Why? Because it is only the extended time that we give to prayer in private that will produce immediate manifestations in short public prayers. We see this clearly demonstrated in the life and ministry of Jesus: His public prayers were short and commanding but His private devotion to God was for a protracted and extended period.

> We have a record of Jesus praying for one hour when He was in the Garden of Gethsemane.

*Then cometh Jesus with them unto a place called Gethsemane, and saith unto the disciples, **Sit ye here, while I go and pray yonder**. And he took with him Peter and the two sons of Zebedee, and began to be sorrowful and very heavy. Then saith he unto them, My soul is exceeding sorrowful, even unto death: tarry ye here, and watch with me. And he went a little further, and fell on his face, and prayed, saying, O my Father, if it be possible, let this cup pass from me: nevertheless not as I will, but as thou wilt. And he cometh unto the disciples, and findeth them asleep, and saith unto Peter, **What, could ye not watch with me one hour**?*

MATTHEW 26:36-40

> We have a record of Jesus praying for three hours.

*And they came to a place which was named Gethsemane: and he saith to his disciples, **Sit ye here, while I shall pray**. And he taketh with him Peter and James and John, and began to be sore amazed, and to be very heavy; And saith unto them, My soul is exceeding sorrowful unto death: **tarry ye here, and watch. And he went forward a little, and fell on the ground, and prayed** that, if it were possible, the hour might pass from him. And he said, Abba, Father, all things are possible unto thee; take away this cup from me: nevertheless not what I will, but what thou wilt.*

And he cometh, and findeth them sleeping, and saith unto Peter, Simon, sleepest thou? **couldest not thou watch one hour? Watch ye and pray,** *lest ye enter into temptation. The spirit truly is ready, but the flesh is weak.* **And again he went away, and prayed, and spake the same words.** *And when he returned, he found them asleep again, (for their eyes were heavy,) neither wist they what to answer him.* **And he cometh the third time,** *and saith unto them, Sleep on now, and take your rest: it is enough, the hour is come;*

MARK 14:32-41

In the Garden of Gethsemane, Jesus was on a prayer watch. As I already mentioned, a *watch* in the Bible is a segment of three hours. Jesus prayed for the first hour and then interacted with his disciples who were a short distance away. Then He came back the second hour and still found them sleepy and then He prayed and pressed through the third hour before He was arrested. Therefore we know He prayed for a three hour watch in the Garden of Gethsemane. When there was pressure, Jesus pressed through in prayer to God.

〉 We have a record of Jesus praying for nine hours

And straightway Jesus constrained his disciples to get into a ship, and to go before him unto the other side, while he sent the multitudes away. And when he had sent the multitudes away, he went up into a mountain apart to pray: and when the evening was come, he was there alone. But the ship was now in the midst of the sea, tossed with waves: for the wind was contrary. And in the fourth watch of the night Jesus went unto them, walking on the sea.

MATTHEW 14:22-25

After a great miracle and healing crusade, as well as the feeding of the five thousand, Jesus *constrained* His disciples to get into a ship to travel to the other side. The word 'constrained' is the Greek word '*anagkazo*' meaning *to compel or force someone toward a particular course of action.* This suggests that the disciples were not in the mood to travel back by ship that evening – after a demanding crusade and feeding five thousand people. This is perfectly understandable as they would have been tired. However Jesus forced them to leave and the multitude also; He personally demanded and assisted the crowd to leave. Why was he so adamant for the crowd and disciples to leave? Here's the answer, '*And when he had sent the multitudes away, he went up into a mountain apart to pray: and when the evening was come, he was there alone...*' Jesus wanted to be alone with God so He deliberately cleared the way. I want you to notice that when evening came He was alone with God in prayer. This would mean that Jesus was ready for the Maariv prayer (Jewish evening prayer time) which started at 6pm. He cleared the crowd and the disciples away in order to keep His prayer time and the next thing we see is that He is walking on the sea in the fourth watch of the night. This watch is the hours between three and six o'clock in the morning so if He started at six in the evening and was heading to the disciples at sea between 3am and 6am then we can deduce that Jesus had prayed for a minimum of nine hours. After these nine hours of praying He was doing the impossible by walking on the water.

> We have a record of Jesus praying all night to God.

*And it came to pass in those days, that he went out into a mountain to pray, and continued all night in prayer to God. **And when it was day, he called unto him his disciples:** and of them he chose twelve, whom also he named apostles; Simon, (whom he also named Peter,) and Andrew his brother, James and John, Philip and Bartholomew, Matthew and Thomas, James the son of Alphæus, and Simon called Zelotes, And Judas the brother of James, and Judas Iscariot, which also was the traitor. **And he came down with them, and stood in the plain, and the company of his disciples, and a great multitude of people out of all Judæa and Jerusalem, and from the sea coast of Tyre and Sidon, which came to hear him, and to be healed of their diseases; And they that were vexed with unclean*** *spirits: and they were healed. And the whole multitude sought to touch him: for there went virtue out of him, and healed them all.*

LUKE 6:12-19

Jesus spent many nights in prayer to God. This was the secret to His life. Jesus pulled an all-night prayer session just before making one of His most important decisions. This decision would be so crucial (it would affect destinies for generations until the present day) that it caused him to seek the mind of God all night long on this matter. This decision was the choosing of His apostles, the commissioned ones that will enable Him to fulfill His destiny and mission.

We need to pray much before we make important decisions. Additionally, when He came down from the mountain of prayer, He was so charged with the virtue of God that they had a healing and deliverance session in the valley. In fact He was so charged with power after His all night session of prayer that the Bible declared that all who came to Him received a tangible touch: '*And the whole multitude sought to touch him: for there went virtue out of him, and healed them all*' (Luke 6:19).

Pray much before you make important decisions
that will affect your destiny

> **We have a record of Jesus praying for forty days and forty nights**

And immediately the Spirit driveth him into the wilderness. And he was there in the wilderness forty days, tempted of Satan; and was with the wild beasts; and the angels ministered unto him.

MARK 1:12-13

And Jesus returned in the power of the Spirit into Galilee: and there went out a fame of him through all the region round about

LUKE 4:14

After forty days of prayer and fasting, Jesus returned fully clothed with the power of God. He launched His public ministry after a forty day prayer and fasting marathon. His ministry's introduction to His home town and the rest of Israel was explosive with manifestations of the miraculous.

Learning to spend long stretches of time before God in prayer and communion can only be a good thing in your life. It will mold you into the image of Christ and build character in you. The whole idea is to spend time with God. The secret to spending a long stretch of time with God is to start where you are. If you have never spent one hour in prayer, don't fool yourself to think you can spend that time on your first effort! Pray fifteen minutes and learn something from it; pray thirty minutes and learn something form it. Consistency is the secret to developing a long stretch of time in prayer. I am grateful that I grew up in a praying church that hosted all night prayer meetings on Fridays from 10 pm till 5 am. I was a teenager when I attended my first all night prayer service and I must admit it was a struggle to stay awake. Sometimes I would fall asleep but I was OK with that because I was happy to be in church. Over time I learnt to press through and prayed all night long. Having friends and pastors who were zealous for prayer helped me engage my prayer life to deeper dimensions. Reading books on the subject also helped a lot.

When you give extended time to prayer in private
it will give you immediate manifestation in short public prayers

CHAPTER 3
THE PRAYER LIFE OF JESUS - PART TWO

WE have been looking at the prayer life of Jesus to extract secrets that we can add to ours. There is no better example than our Lord after whom we should fashion our own prayer life. His time on the earth was saturated with prayer and it would be wise on our part to also saturate our lives with this great weapon at our disposal.

૭ Jesus wielded prayer to PULL DOWN PRINCIPALITIES AND POWERS

Jesus did not simply view prayer as a form of communication or fellowship with His Father. To Him, prayer was also a weapon in His arsenal to deal with the devil. Prayer in the life of Jesus was not just romancing God but wrestling with principalities and powers to pull them down so they no longer influenced the atmosphere and cities where He would minister. *Prayer is spiritual warfare.* After Jesus spent forty days and forty nights in prayer and fasting, Luke writes an interesting observation:

And Jesus returned in the power of the Spirit into Galilee: and there went out a fame of him through all the region round about.

LUKE 4:14

Now we think this fame is talking about the natural regions of Nazareth, Galilee and Judea. How could that be the case when He had not even preached His first message or cast a devil out? This verse speaks of the *spiritual* regions. In the realm of the spirit – the unseen realm – the demons and principalities knew there was a new sheriff in town; they could no longer influence the spiritual and natural regions as they used to. A stronger man had come in to spoil the goods (Luke 11:22). We see this scenario repeated with the mad man of Gadara. Both Mark and Luke recorded this event. Here is a summary of what happened.

Prayer is spiritual warfare

Jesus and his disciples came by ship to the other side of the lake, to the region of the Gadarenes. As He was getting out of the boat, a man with an evil spirit quickly ran to Him from the cemetery where he had been living. That man was so demonized he had often been put in chains and leg irons, but he broke the chains and smashed the leg irons. No one and nothing could control him. Day and night he remained in the graveyard, yelling, squealing in torment and cutting himself with stones. He was some distance away when he saw Jesus; so he ran, fell on his knees before Him, and screamed in a loud voice, *'Jesus, Son of the Most High God! What do you want with me?'* Jesus had already commanded, *'Come out of this man, you evil spirit!'* Then Jesus asked him, *'What is your name?'*

The man answered, *'My name is Legion, because I have many spirits in me.'* The spirits in the man begged Jesus again and again not to send them out of that area. A large herd of pigs was feeding on a mountainside nearby. The demons kept begging Jesus, *'Send us into the pigs! Let us enter them!'* Jesus let them do this. The evil spirits came out of the man and went into the pigs. The herd of about two thousand pigs rushed down the cliff into the sea and drowned. Those who tended the pigs ran away and retold the event in the city and countryside. People came to see what had happened. They came to Jesus and saw the man who used to be demonized sitting there fully dressed and completely free and of a sound mine. All the people of the city pleaded with Jesus to leave their region. Jesus did not argue with them: He left. The man who was once demonized went to Jesus and asked if he could travel with Him and be part of his crew of disciples but Jesus told him to go and tell what God has done for him. The next thing he did is that he went to Decapolis – meaning ten cities – and spread the good news of how Jesus had delivered him. Now notice what happened next:

And he departed, and began to publish in Decapolis how great things Jesus had done for him: and all men did marvel. And when Jesus was passed over again by ship unto the other side, much people gathered unto him: and he was nigh unto the sea.

MARK 5:20-21

And it came to pass, that, when Jesus was returned, the people gladly received him: for they were all waiting for him

LUKE 8:40

Jesus dealt with the principality over Gadara. It was a stronghold and nobody had any influence except the demon spirit in that man who lived in the tomb. Jesus took authority over it and when He came back again, the same crowd which refused Him before now welcomed Him, expecting great miracles. Why? Because Jesus possessed the gates of His enemies through strong prayer. He did it before he stepped into full time ministry and He did it in Gadara. He shifted the heavens with His prayers. Don't get the idea that Jesus had everything easy for Him because He was God manifested in the flesh: Jesus operated as a man, anointed with the Holy Spirit –just like us! Everything He did on the earth was as an anointed man showing us how we can operate in this earth. This is why He was constantly in prayer because prayer creates a shift in the realm of the spirit. It dethrones principalities and powers who reign unchallenged in cities and nations.

Prayer in the life of Jesus was not just romancing God but wrestling with principalities and powers to pull them down

---

You really need to grasp that prayer is a weapon of mass destruction in the camp of the enemy. It was through prayer and consistency of prayer, coupled with fasting that Daniel shifted the Prince of Persia. Like Jesus, Daniel and Paul we also need to pray and create a shift in the spirit realm so that we do not live and function in ministry subject to the controlling powers of principalities over our regions. Paul told us that the weapons of our warfare are not carnal but mighty through God to the pulling down of strongholds. There are spiritual strongholds of wickedness over your city.

29

What are you going to do about it? Don't sit there discouraged and say, 'Ohhh this is a hard place, nobody gets saved and healed here.' Didn't the Bible tell you to break up the fallow ground (Hosea 10:12)? Yes, it did! You will do so in prayer. Rise up in prayer and pull down the strongholds of the enemy.

You need to let the devil know there is a new sheriff in town who does not back down from anything. There are wicked strongholds over your family line. What are you going to do about it? Don't look at your loved ones helplessly and say, 'it is just part of my family line.' No! Be like Jesus, spend time in intercessory prayer, the kind of prayer that knocks down walls, bulldozing every opposition and flattens the long erected walls of resistance. You can pull down the wicked strongholds with prayer and violent faith. Remember Jesus said, '*The violent takes it by force*' (Matthew 11:12). We will have a chapter looking more in depth at the warfare and contending aspect of prayer.

Prayer creates a shift in the realm of the spirit

Jesus advocated PERSISTENCE in prayer

And he spake a parable unto them to this end, that men ought always to pray, and not to faint

LUKE 18:1

And being in an agony he prayed more earnestly: *and his sweat was as it were great drops of blood falling down to the ground. And when he rose up from prayer, and was come to his disciples, he found them sleeping for sorrow*

LUKE 22:44-45

When Jesus was in agony of mind, he persisted in prayer. He did not surrender and faint. He persisted and pressed in prayer until He broke through. The old timers used to call this kind of prayer, 'Praying through' which is something we need to learn to do in the modern church. Jesus also revealed to us the different dimensions of prayer when he said, '*Ask, and it shall be given you; seek, and ye shall find; knock, and it shall be opened unto you*' (Matthew 7:7). I really like the way the Amplified Bible puts it which is what the Greek text expresses:

Ask and keep on asking and it will be given to you; seek and keep on seeking and you will find; knock and keep on knocking and the door will be opened to you..

MATTHEW 7:7

The Lord was well aware that our prayers would be resisted by the enemy. God is not your problem but the devil and his cohorts certainly are. They will endeavor to put roadblocks to your blessings. The enemy will try to impose a spiritual embargo on your life, ministry and destiny. This is why Jesus revealed the three dimensions and depths of prayer: *Ask*, *seek* and *knock*. If you don't get it by asking, don't get discouraged, seek for it. If you don't get it by seeking, then there is a wall of opposition: knock it down with aggressive praying.

Jesus knew there would be spiritual embargos, delay tactics and roadblocks to our prayers and this is why He kept teaching on persistence in prayers. He taught the disciples the *prayer of importunity*. He also taught the disciples about the widow and the unrighteous judge. The continual, persistent asking by this widow got her what she desired. Can the same be said of your prayers? This widow's tenacity became more weighty and more influential than the most powerful political figures and although the unjust judge had no regard *for* her, he was forced to yield *to* her. Then Jesus made a contrast in the application, in respect to God, the Righteous Judge and his elect that are incessant in their petitions.

Jesus posed a question and showed us the contrast of characters, '*And shall not God avenge his own elect, which cry day and night unto him,*

though he bear long with them? I tell you that he will avenge them speedily.
Nevertheless when the Son of man cometh, shall he find faith on the earth?'
(Luke 18:7-8). Jesus informed us that if we do not quit and surrender, God
will avenge us quicker than we think.

All the characters in these parables were rewarded because of their dogged
determination or persistence in prayer! Jesus said that persistence in prayer
is undergirded by faith. You need to understand that prayer is an expression
of faith and faith is the foundation of your prayer. Later in the book, we
will look at the *prayer of importunity* and persistent prayer in more detail.

Persistence breaks resistance

Jesus prayed with PASSION

Who in the days of his flesh, when he had offered up prayers and
supplications with strong crying and tears unto him that was able to
save him from death, and was heard in that he feared .

HEBREWS 5:7

Jesus was not lackadaisical in prayer. Many times when we pray, we
have a lackluster attitude and we wonder why prayer is boring. Prayer is
boring because you are boring; whatever attitude you bring to prayer is
exactly how it will reflect back to you. In the above verse, we see there was
fervor in the prayers of Jesus. His prayers were with strong crying and tears.
At other times, it was with a loud voice or a commanding decree, as before
Lazarus' grave. For the multiplication of bread, He simply looked up to
heaven. In His prayer recorded in John 17, Jesus also looked up to heaven
and conversed long with God. In the Garden of Gethsemane, He knelt down
and agonized in prayer. The point I am driving in you is that Jesus was all
wrapped up in His prayers at different situations.

He knew how to posture himself. The reason we become discouraged in
prayer is because we think there is only one way or one mode of prayer.

Some people think that prayer is constantly shouting, so they shout at God all the way through until they wear themselves out. Others have the idea that prayer is total silence before God. If that is all you have been exposed to, it is not surprising that you find prayer boring. You cannot keep shouting all the time, nor can you be in total silence every time you pray: it will be monotonous and mundane and you will not sustain it. Just like you have different emotions, prayer also has different emotions, modes and scopes. Just as there are different ranges in voices there are different ranges in prayer.

Prayer is boring because you are boring; whatever attitude you bring to prayer is exactly how it will reflect back to you

Your personality and culture also play a part in the way you posture yourself to pray. I am a naturally loud-mouthed islander, born in Mauritius who grew up in England, raised among African believers (mainly Nigerians and Ghanaians) and was heavily influenced by charismatic American ministers, so the idea of total silence at all times in prayer does not resonate with me. There are times when I pray silently but I am more of an extrovert personality. My wife, on the other hand is less inclined to be as vocal as I am; nonetheless there is just as much fervor in her prayers as in mine. When I am praying in the Holy Room in my house, the whole family can hear me and I do not care. When my wife is praying by herself, only God can hear her. I am not better than her and she is not better than me. Fervency in our prayer is all that matters; it's not a matter of tone and decibel but a matter of the heart. You can be an introvert and still be fervent in prayer. The introvert's passion and fervor will be different in expression from the extrovert's, nonetheless it is still passion and fervor. Hannah's prayer to break barrenness and give birth to Samuel was full of faith and fervor but look at how she prayed:

Now Hannah, she spake in her heart; only her lips moved, but her voice was not heard:

1 SAMUEL 1:13

To a lot of Charismatics and Pentecostals that does not sound like passion and fervency because our expression of fervency is to bring the house down by praying up a storm, with spit flying, hand gesturing, voice raising and vein-throbbing prayer.

*Fervency is not a matter of tone and decibel
but a matter of the heart*

Jesus prayed His most passionate prayers in the toughest spots. Here are three examples of the different expressions of the passion of Jesus in prayer.

⟩ Jairus' Daughter

Jairus had come specifically to draw Jesus to his house because his twelve year old daughter was at the point of death. On the way there, Jesus was delayed because a woman with an issue of blood pressed through the crowd and drew power out of Jesus for her healing. That caused Jesus to stop and pose the question, '*Who touched me?*' Finally the woman came and testified. While all this was going on (and time being an important element), Jairus received word that his daughter was dead. At which point Jesus immediately looked at him and said, '*Fear not, only believe.*' Jesus then followed Jairus all the way to his house and by the time he got there the wailers were busy wailing her death. Jesus removed all of them, went into the room, took the girl by the hand and calmly said, '*Talitha Cumi*' meaning 'little girl arise' (Mark 5). **Jesus was calm but yet authoritative over death.**

⟩ Lazarus' grave

Lazarus and his two sisters, Mary and Martha loved Jesus and were very close to Him. When Lazarus fell ill, his sisters sent word to Jesus about Lazarus' plight. Jesus stayed two more days where He was after He heard the news and by the time He arrived at Lazarus' place, the latter had been dead for four days already. Martha ran ahead and met Jesus and a little later Mary also ran to meet the Master sorrowing and crying. When Jesus saw the tears and sorrow of Mary, *he was moved and he groaned in the spirit* and was stirred. Jesus then wept and groaned further in the spirit. He then gently talked to His Father, thanking Him that He had already heard His prayer and followed it with a loud command, '*Lazarus come forth*', to which the latter responded even though he had been dead for four days and was already decomposing and stinking (John 11). In this situation we see Jesus expressed His passion by groaning in prayer, weeping, talking to the Father and commanding death to let go. There were different expressions of passion in the same situation.

⟩ Garden of Gethsemane

Jesus was now under heavy pressure. He was about to be made the sin offering that would take away the sin of the world. In the natural the pressure was severe, to the point He was sweating blood, but He obeyed and prayed for the will of God to be done:

> *And he went a little further, and fell on his face, and prayed, saying, O my Father, if it be possible, let this cup pass from me: nevertheless not as I will, but as thou wilt*

> MATTHEW 26:39

His expression of passion in prayer was to fall on His face before His Father. He was not limited to one type of emotion and neither will you be, so don't confine yourself to one type of prayer. The more you pray the more expressions of the different passions of prayer you will experience. Let your prayers be full of fire and fervor no matter what type of person you are.

It is in the privacy of prayer that we develop intimacy with God. Then intimacy triggers accuracy in the Spirit

♪ Jesus taught us that prayer is PARTURITION

Parturition simply means the act or process of giving birth to offspring. A great aspect of prayer is travailing and giving birth to souls, dreams and destinies. Travailing prayer is becoming a lost art in the church as we have moved from waiting on the Lord to quick fix schemes and secular marketing to fill the church. While marketing has a place, the way that the church is filled is by travailing and laboring in prayer for souls. Jesus taught us to travail in prayer until we give birth to our destinies. Jesus labored and travailed in prayer in the Garden of Gethsemane for the birthing of God's mission. When pressure and fear would have wanted Him to abort the mission, Jesus pressed through the pain in prayer. Now see what the great prophet Isaiah said:

*He shall see of the **travail of his soul,** and shall be satisfied: by his knowledge shall my righteous servant justify many; for he shall bear their iniquities. Therefore will I divide him a portion with the great, and he shall divide the spoil with the strong; because he hath poured out his soul unto death: and he was numbered with the transgressors; and he bare the sin of many, and **made intercession for the transgressors.***

ISAIAH 53:11-12

*A normal parturition occurs in a private setup
in order not to freak out others*

The fifty-third chapter of Isaiah of the Suffering Servant is Messianic in content and unveils the work of Calvary's Cross hundreds of years before Jesus appeared on the scene. Notice, part of His priestly duties was travailing and intercession for souls. Travailing prayer brings forth birth; there will not be any birth without travailing. This is what we call natal prayer and we will learn more about it in the chapter on the dimensions and depths of prayer from Jesus.

According to the author of Hebrews, Jesus brought many sons to glory (Hebrews 2:10). He did so by Calvary's Cross and His ever present intercession.

Both Paul and Epaphras travailed in prayer for the churches they were responsible over (Galatians 4:19, Colossians 4).

The travailing prayer of Hannah produced a long awaited son in her life. Our parturitional prayer will also produce spiritual sons. A normal parturition occurs in a private setup in order not to freak out others. Just as babies are born in private, most birthing of spiritual things are also achieved in the privacy of the prayer closet, which I call the labor ward. Let us allow the Lord Jesus to define to us parturition and travailing prayer:

> *Verily, I say unto you, That ye shall weep and lament, but the world shall rejoice: and ye shall be sorrowful, but your sorrow shall be turned into joy. A woman when she is in travail hath sorrow, because her hour is come: but as soon as she is delivered of the child, she remembereth no more the anguish, for joy that a man is born into the world. And ye now therefore have sorrow: but I will see you again, and your heart shall rejoice, and your joy no man taketh from you.*
>   JOHN 16:20-22

Remember this response is after Jesus had told His disciples they would not see Him for a little while but that they would be indwelt by the Holy Spirit. The indwelling of the Spirit will turn their sorrow into joy and Jesus equates this sorrow and joy to a woman giving birth. Why? This gives us a big pointer to one of the works of the Holy Spirit in our lives which is to help us birth and add new believers to the church.

Parturition, which consists of travailing, laboring, pains, contractions and pangs is distressing but once the delivery takes place there is joy. This is why Paul said of the Holy Spirit, '*Likewise the Spirit also helpeth our infirmities: for we know not what we should **pray for as we ought**: but the Spirit itself maketh **intercession for us with groanings** which cannot be uttered. And he that searcheth the hearts knoweth what is the mind of the Spirit, because he maketh intercession for the saints according to the will of God*' (Romans:26-27).

When we travail in prayer we will experience and connect with: '*They that sow in tears shall reap in joy. He that goeth forth and weepeth, bearing precious seed, shall doubtless come again with rejoicing, bringing his sheaves with him*' (Psalm 126:5-6).

A woman in labour is in pain but the end product is joy, new life and productivity. Parturition prayer brings in new life, joy and productivity to our ministries and churches.

§ Jesus prayed for PEOPLE AND FOR HIS OWN PERSON

Jesus was an example of how we should pray. Apart from His praying for the sick and afflicted, Jesus also prayed for His disciples and for Himself. In John 17, we see a great example of Jesus praying for Himself and His disciples and for His future disciples. We also see that he prayed for Peter:

> *And the Lord said, Simon, Simon, behold, Satan hath desired to have you, that he may sift you as wheat: But I have prayed for thee, that thy faith fail not: and when thou art converted, strengthen thy brethren.*
>
> LUKE 22:31-32

Jesus teaches us that we can pray and intercede for our friends and loved ones. Through His prayer, Jesus stopped the desire of Satan. If Jesus had not prayed and interceded for Peter, he would have been a castaway. That should stir us to pray for our loved ones. When you see your children vacillating in their faith, you can pray for them that their faith does not fail. We need to keep in mind the words of the Prophet Samuel:

> *Moreover as for me, God forbid that I should sin against the Lord in ceasing to pray for you: but I will teach you the good and the right way*
>
> 1 SAMUEL 12:23

In the mind of Samuel it would be a sin if he did not pray for his people. Parents need to pray for their children; if they don't who else will? Pastors need to pray for their congregation; if they don't who else will. The apostle Paul was constantly praying for the churches that he planted.

See what Paul said to the Galatian churches:

My little children, of whom I travail in birth again until Christ be formed in you
GALATIANS 4:19

Parents, do you travail in prayer over your children until Christ is formed in them? Pastors, instead of griping about your congregation's lack of sanctification, have you travailed in intercessory prayer until Christ is formed in them? See what Paul said of Epaphras:

Epaphras, who is one of you, a servant of Christ, saluteth you, always labouring fervently for you in prayers, that ye may stand perfect and complete in all the will of God.
COLOSSIANS 4:12

Epaphras labored fervently in prayers for the Colossian saints to stand perfect in the will of God. This is what Jesus did for His disciples, Paul did for his churches and Epaphras did for the Colossian saints. You really need to add this to your repertoire in prayer.

We see Jesus praying for Himself all through the Gospels. In John 17, the priestly prayer of Jesus was threefold:

1. He prayed for Himself.
2. He prayed for His disciples.
3. He prayed for future and all believers, which means *you* are included.

Jesus showed us it is important to pray for ourselves. Some people pride themselves in the fact that they never pray for themselves. This is not smart and is why so many find their destinies delayed. Here is a great example of someone who prayed for himself:

*And Jabez was more honourable than his brethren: and his mother called his name Jabez, saying, Because I bare him with sorrow. **And Jabez called*** *on the God of Israel, saying, Oh that thou wouldest bless me indeed, and enlarge my coast, and that thine hand might be with me, and that thou wouldest keep me from evil, that it may not grieve me! And God granted him that which he requested.*

1 Chronicles 4:9-10

The prayer that you do not pray is the prayer that will not be answered. God cannot answer what you do not ask for. To quote John Wesley, '*It seems God is limited by our prayer life. God can do nothing for humanity unless someone asks Him.*' This is not just talking about praying for your city or nation but for yourself also. If Jabez did not pray for himself, his verse in the Bible would just be, '*And Jabez was more honourable than his brethren: and his mother called his name Jabez, saying, Because I bare him with sorrow.*' That would have been the end; all he would have going for himself would be the fact that he was honorable but his life was sorrowful.

This is where so many millions of believers are today. They are honorable, they love God but their lives are bitter with sorrow. However Jabez changed the trajectory of his life by praying for himself. Look at his prayer, '*Oh that thou wouldest bless me indeed, and enlarge my coast, and that thine hand might be with me, and that thou wouldest keep me from evil, that it may not grieve me!*'

❖ Bless me indeed.
❖ Enlarge my coast.
❖ Your hand be with me.
❖ Keep me from evil.

Jabez prayed for God to empower him to prosper. Are you praying for God to empower you to prosper? Secondly he prayed that God would enlarge his coast. He did not want any limitations upon him. You should pray for God to enlarge your borders and influence. Thirdly you need to pray for God's hand of favor to be with you. Every time the Bible mentions the hand of God it always refers to the miraculous. So we need to ask God for the miraculous.

Fourthly, you need to pray for God's protection to keep you from evil. If both Jesus and Jabez prayed for themselves then you need to pray for yourself. For many years I have been praying Paul's prayer for the Ephesians and Colossians on a personal basis. The Ephesian prayer is for revelation and the Colossians prayer is for direction and provision:

Cease not to give thanks for you, making mention of you in my prayers; That the God of our Lord Jesus Christ, the Father of glory, may give unto you the spirit of wisdom and revelation in the knowledge of him: The eyes of your understanding being enlightened; that ye may know what is the hope of his calling, and what the riches of the glory of his inheritance in the saints, And what is the exceeding greatness of his power to us-ward who believe, according to the working of his mighty power, Which he wrought in Christ, when he raised him from the dead, and set him at his own right hand in the heavenly places, Far above all principality, and power, and might, and dominion, and every name that is named, not only in this world, but also in that which is to come: And hath put all things under his feet, and gave him to be the head over all things to the church, Which is his body, the fulness of him that filleth all in all.
EPHESIANS 1:16-23

For this cause we also, since the day we heard it, do not cease to pray for you, and to desire that ye might be filled with the knowledge of his will in all wisdom and spiritual understanding; That ye might walk worthy of the Lord unto all pleasing, being fruitful in every good work, and increasing in the knowledge of God; Strengthened with all might, according to his glorious power, unto all patience and longsuffering with joyfulness;
COLOSSIANS 1:9-11

The prayer that you do not pray is the prayer that will not be answered

---

For years my prayer confession has been:

'*Father I thank you that the God of my Lord Jesus Christ, the Father of glory, has given unto me the spirit of wisdom and revelation in the knowledge of Christ*

The eyes of my understanding and spirit have been enlightened and flooded with lights

I know what is the hope of my calling, and what the riches of the glory of God's inheritance in the saints

I understand and grasp the exceeding greatness of your power to me who believes, according to the working of your mighty power

Which you wrought in Christ, when you raised Him from the dead, and set Him at His own right hand in the heavenly places

Far above all principality, avnd power, and might, and dominion, and every name that is named, not only in this world, but also in that which is to come

And hath put all things under His feet, and gave Him to be the head over all things to the church, Which is His body, the fulness of Him that filleth all in all

Now my Father, I thank you that I am filled with the knowledge of your will in all wisdom and spiritual understanding

Enabling me to walk worthy of the Lord unto all pleasing

I am fruitful and productive in every good work and I come behind in no gift

I am increasing in the knowledge of God and I am strengthened with all might, according to his glorious power, unto all patience and longsuffering with joyfulness

I praise and thank you Father for my redemption in Christ.'

◈ Jesus taught us PREPARATION is needful in prayer

We can say much more on the prayer life of Jesus but I am going to end this chapter with a great key to an effective and fruitful prayer life. The reason we struggle to pray for any good length of time is because we are *not prepared*. There is more to developing a consistent prayer life than just loving and romancing God. Failing to prepare is preparing to fail. You need to understand the different rules of engagement when it comes to prayer. We think that we can wing it but unfortunately because we are not structured and prepared in the set up of prayer we become disillusioned with our prayer life and cannot sustain what we start. It is like going to the gym and doing everything without any plan: you will not see effective results.

When the disciples asked Jesus to teach them on prayer, He gave them a model. Traditionally it has been called *the Lord's prayer* but technically the Lord's prayer is found in John 17 and in the Garden of Gethsemane. What we call the Lord's prayer is really a model prayer – a modus operandi – meaning a particular way or method of doing something, especially one that is characteristic or well-established.

Let's briefly look at the model prayer:

After this manner therefore pray ye: Our Father which art in heaven, Hallowed be thy name. Thy kingdom come. Thy will be done in earth, as it is in heaven. Give us this day our daily bread. And forgive us our debts, as we forgive our debtors. And lead us not into temptation, but deliver us from evil: For thine is the kingdom, and the power, and the glory, for ever. Amen.

MATTHEW 6:9-13

Basically Jesus was giving us a guideline how to pray:

1. **Our Father** –Acknowledging God as the Supreme Being and our Father, the Creator and source of all life. The fact that we address Him as Father means we are now in His family, redeemed because of the blood of Jesus.

2. **Which art in heaven** – God is in the historic past, present and the future and He reigns from heaven above all powers and principalities.

3. **Hallowed be thy name** – Praise and Worship. Exalt and confess the redemptive names of God. We are told that God inhabits the praises of His people (Psalm 22:3) and that we are to enter His gates with praise and thanksgiving (Psalms 100:4). We praise and extol the redemptive names of God and His other powerful names revealing His character and attributes: These names are holy.

We can find the Redemptive names of God from Psalm 23:

❖ **Jehovah Ra-ah** – The Lord our shepherd – *The Lord is my shepherd* (Psalm 23:1).

❖ **Jehovah Jireh** – The Lord our provider – *I shall not want* (Psalm 23:1, Genesis 22:13,14).

❖ **Jehovah Shalom** – The Lord our peace – *He maketh me to lie down in green pastures: he leadeth me beside the still waters* (Psalm 23:2, Judges 44:24).

❖ **Jehovah Rapha** – the Lord our healer – *He restoreth my soul* (Psalm 23:3, Exodus 15:26).

❖ **Jehovah Tsidkenu** – The Lord our righteousness – *He leadeth me in the paths of righteousness for his name's sake* (Psalm 23:3, Jeremiah 23:6).

❖ **Jehovah Nissi** – The Lord My Banner – *Yea, though I walk through the valley of the shadow of death, I will fear no evil: for thou art with me; thy rod and thy staff they comfort me.*

❖ **Jehovah M'Kaddesh** – The Lord our sanctifier – *Thou preparest a table before me in the presence of mine enemies: thou anointest my head with oil; my cup runneth over* (Psalm 23:4,5, Exodus 31:13).

❖ **Jehovah Shammah** – The Lord is there/ever present – I will fear no evil: for thou art with me; (Psalm 23:4, Ezekiel 48:35).

There are other names of God that you can engage in your prayer time. Allow me to mention a few but you can do more research and engage other names of God for the manifestations of these facets of God in your life:

❖ **El Shaddai** – Almighty God, the Breasted One, He who reserves the right to undo nature, reverse and accelerate the laws of nature.
❖ **El Elyon** – The Most High God.
❖ **Adonai** – Lord, Master.
❖ **Jehovah Sabaoth** – The Lord of Hosts who fights for you and will decapitate the head of your enemies.

4. **Thy kingdom come. Thy will be done on earth as it is in heaven** – Pray for the will of God to be established upon the earth in your life, family, church, city and nation.
5. **Give us this day our daily bread** – Pray for provision.
6. **And forgive us our debts, as we forgive our debtors** – Pray to stay free from offense and sin that easily besets us.
7. **And lead us not into temptation, but deliver us from evil** – Pray for divine protection.
8. **For thine is the kingdom, and the power, and the glory, for ever** – End with praising God's greatness.

Using this model you can pray for one hour to three hours and in-between each prayer point, pray in the Spirit in your heavenly language, then revert to praying in your known language. Prayer isn't a performance but let us remember the old motivational quote, '*The quality of your preparation determines the quality of your performance.*' If you want to perform well in prayer then you must prepare. **Preparation time is not wasted time.**

If you want to go to another model apart from the Lord's prayer, many years ago Dr Yonggi Cho, a great man of prayer taught on the 'Tabernacle Prayer' which is a wonderful resource that you can tap into and implement in your life. Among many other models, here is a personal model that I use in my prayer arsenal.

> ### ⟩ Prayer model in my personal life

Firstly, I pray for the strengthening of my inner and outer man. I need to be both strong spiritually and physically. So I pray in the Spirit to strengthen my spirit and I confess the Word. I go through certain Scripture references in the Bible such as the prayers of Paul in Ephesians and Colossians and confess them. I pray the Ephesians prayer for wisdom, revelation and dominion (Ephesians 1:16-23). I pray the Colossians prayer to know the will of God and for the provision to follow (Colossians 1:9-11). Nothing is worse than vision without provision. Tongues and confession play a great part in my prayer life; I give much time to praying in the Spirit in regards to walking in revelation. This is very important to me. God has called me into the office of a teacher and evangelist therefore I must be loaded with revelation and power. I am not satisfied to read a book and rehash what someone else has said however great that may be so I pray and push in the Spirit, studying the Word, expecting God to open another vista of His Word and for His power to manifest when I'm preaching or teaching.

Tongues and confession play a great part in my prayer life

Secondly, I pray for my wife and children. One by one I call their names before God. I pray in the Spirit over them and then boldly declare the Promises of God over them. I do this *every day*.

Thirdly, I Pray for the ministry. I constantly pray for the opening of three doors: the door of utterance, the door of faith and the door of ministry. This is what gives a minister influence in the earth. I need the door of utterance to effectively express the revelations God gives me. I need the door of faith to release the miracles, signs and wonders in the meetings. I need the door of ministry to walk through influential doors. Therefore between each prayer point for each door, I pray in tongues and make bold decrees. This can continue for a few minutes, an hour or hours. You see for years I focused on the teaching aspect of my ministry but the Lord spoke to me one night and said, '*You have given your time and attention to the teaching ministry. You have been faithful to dispense the revelational Word but you must also give time to the work of the evangelist. For there is a dearth of evangelists in the land.*'

Fourthly, I pray against witchcraft and spiritual opposition. This is a very important part of my prayer life. As Moses was resisted by Jannes and Jambres, Nehemiah was resisted by Sanballat and Tobiah, Daniel was resisted by the Prince of Persia, Jesus was resisted by the Pharisees and Saduccees and Paul was resisted by Elymas the sorcerer, I realize there are spiritual forces, opposition and witchcraft delaying my progress in life and ministry. My head is not buried in the sand thinking the devil will not oppose me: he is my adversary. The word 'adversary' is the Greek word *antidikos*, a combination of two words: *anti* meaning 'denying' and 'against' and *dikos* meaning 'rights'. The combination of these two words reveal the plan of the devil, my adversary, to deny me my rights. He is against my rights and against justice being done in my favor. At the same time I am his adversary. I don't wait to be attacked; I pray in the Spirit, then speak in my understanding against every spirit of opposition, binding their operations against my life.

Realize there are spiritual forces, opposition and witchcraft opposing your progress in life and ministry

Even though Moses had a specific word and mission from God, he was resisted by the high level witchcraft of Egypt impeding the rights and deliverance of Israel. You need to realize that witchcraft is real.

Jehu revealed a very important aspect of witchcraft, '*What peace, so long as the whoredoms of thy mother Jezebel and her witchcrafts are so many?*' (2 Kings 9:22). Witchcraft disturbs your peace, prosperity and well being.

Fifthly, I end with praise and worship, making my own song to the Lord or singing one of my favorite praise or worship songs of adoration. I bless Him for His greatness and goodness.

Your preparation in prayer, like Jesus will bear much fruit. As you have learnt the eleven secrets of the prayer life of Jesus, add them to your life and you also will experience long segments of time in God's presence.

CHAPTER 4
DEFINING PRAYER

MANY people have defined prayer, with different meanings and connotations. In this chapter we will look at a simple definition of prayer and focus on it. If you have been in church long enough you may think you know what prayer is because like so many you have taken prayer for granted. You can be raised in church and still don't know what prayer means. You need to realize that in its originality the word *prayer* and the word *pray* were legal words used within the set up of a court. The words associated with prayer – such as petitions, supplications, advocate, adversary, accuser and judge – are all legal words employed in a judicial system. Nowadays, due to the fact that we associate the word prayer with church, religion and asking God for things, we have not comprehended the legalities and constitutionalities of prayer. We have diluted and oversimplified prayer.

Firstly, I am sure you have heard people say, 'prayer is making your request before God.' While this is absolutely true, prayer is not just a shopping list to take before the Creator of the Universe. Indeed, God is our provider, He is our Jehovah Jireh who desires to meet our petitions, supplications, and intercessions but there is more to prayer than just a shopping list.

Secondly, you will have heard people say, 'prayer is just talking to God'. Yes, prayer is conversational, a dialogue between you and your Heavenly Father. God is the master communicator and wants to converse back and forth with you. One of the very first things we learn about God in Genesis is that he talks:

And they heard the voice of the Lord God walking in the garden in the cool of the day...

GENESIS 3:8

God is always talking. We are the ones with the hearing problem but when God speaks He gives direction, instruction and delivers us from pitfalls:

For God speaketh once, yea twice, yet man perceiveth it not. In a dream, in a vision of the night, when deep sleep falleth upon men, in slumberings upon the bed; Then he openeth the ears of men, and sealeth their instruction, That he may withdraw man from his purpose, and hide pride from man. He keepeth back his soul from the pit, and his life from perishing by the sword.

Job 33:14-18

Thirdly, you will have heard that prayer is the deepening of your relationship with God. This is absolutely true. Prayer is fellowshipping with the greatest person ever, the Creator. You will get to know God the more you spend time with Him. Listen to the words of Jesus:

And this is life eternal, that they should know Thee, the only true God

John 17:3

While these are great definitions for prayer – and all of them are valid, enriching your prayer life, I want to look at one that I believe you should grasp in order for you to unleash the full force of your prayer life. To help in this regard I will describe an event that transpired in my life, to give you a mental picture to mark your life and thinking.

The highest result of prayer is not deliverance from evil, or the securing of some coveted thing, but knowledge of God
– Unknown Christian

§ My brother Bruno

My mom and dad have three boys. I am the eldest and the two that followed me are Bruno and James. I am barely one year older than Bruno.

James was the youngest so he was no trouble for me. Bruno on the other hand was a whole different notion. Although I am older than him he was bigger, stronger, and meaner than me when we were growing up. He was meaner than a junkyard dog and could rearrange my face anytime he wanted to. He would also tell you I was meaner than a junkyard dog when I was young. So growing up we tussled many times and he won most of the battles except if I had something in my hands – like AA batteries; then I would throw them at him. One time I wrestled with him, pinned him down and inserted my fingers into his mouth, enlarging it. He was spared by my mom walking in on us. Another time I made him mad and he hit me at the back of my head with his lunch bag – which had a glass bottle in it – and split my head, causing me to need stitches. As you can see, we were pretty rambunctious in our younger years before we were saved. Thank God all this is behind us now!

When we were teenagers growing up in London, England, Bruno had a part time job working in a clothing shop, which meant he had money. I, on the other hand did not have a part time job so money was a bit of an issue for me. With his money, Bruno bought himself some great looking tennis shoes and warned me not touch or wear them. I must admit the temptation was too much for me to bear. I knew he had to go to work on the Saturday and that he would leave the house around 8am to get to work for 9am and be home about 7pm (his job finished at 6pm). So I devised a cunning plan to wear the tennis shoes from 9am (as he would be at work by then) and put them back in the box under his bed by 5pm. That would have given me a buffer zone of two hours. It was a glorious day as everybody admired my tennis shoes! I felt like a million bucks strutting around my friends and neighborhood in London. I returned home about 4pm thinking that my plan was working to a tee. Just after 5pm, I was standing in-between the family room and the kitchen door when all of a sudden the other door to the family room swung open.

Guess who walked through? Bruno!! It was not even 6pm yet and he was home.

Now you need to understand something about my brother, he has a lazy eye when he is angry or tired; one of his eyes goes cockeyed. As we both stood there, one of his eyes was looking at me and the other at the tennis shoes. I couldn't say anything. I froze. He asked, 'Why are you wearing my tennis shoes?' Before I could answer, the guy just walked over and swung a punch at me. He was out to cause a black eye but I managed to swerve, only for his fist to hit my ear and the other ear to hit the door. I was in pain and I did not know which ear to hold. When I held the left ear, there was a sharp pain in the right ear. I was so angry as I was holding my ears that I felt a heat go by my face. I said to myself, 'This is it. Somebody is going to die today. This kitchen is not big enough for the two of us.' So I mustered all my strength and power in my left fist (as I am left handed). I was hoping to land one knockout punch in his eyes to make the other one cockeyed too. As I was coming up to land a great knockout punch to his eye socket, all of a sudden, my mother jumped in-between us. God really helped me that day. Somehow I managed to pull back that punch – for which I am eternally grateful. What did my mother do in stepping in the middle? She intervened. It was an act of intervention stopping an incoming attack.

This is what the word *prayer* or *to pray* means: it is a legal word requesting an intervention. This is a very important truth to grasp. God does things legally. He does not usurp authority nor does He trespass boundaries:

*And God said, **Let us make man** in our image, after our likeness: and **let them have dominion** over the fish of the sea, and over the fowl of the air, and over the cattle, and over all the earth, and over every creeping thing that creepeth upon the earth.*

GENESIS 1:26

Prayer is an act of intervention, raising a wall of defense stopping an incoming attack

God created man with words of dominion and gave them dominion. When God said, 'Let us make man in our image and likeness' He clearly implicated himself in the making of man but then when He said, 'Let them have dominion', He distinctly gave man autonomy and sovereignty over the earth. See what the Psalmist says:

> *The heaven, even the heavens, are the Lord's:* **but the earth hath he given to the children of men.**
>
> PSALM 115:16

Just as it is illegal to invade and impose upon a sovereign nation, God would not invade nor impose Himself upon the jurisdiction and sovereignty of man. This is why prayer is so important. When you pray, you are legally asking a Higher Superpower to intervene in your affairs. Prayer is giving God legal permission to intervene in your life. To pray is to invite God in to your affairs legally. This is why the original understanding of the legal framework of the word *prayer* is vitally important in order for us to secure victory.

Prayer is giving God legal permission to intervene in your life

Prayer is entreating or engaging God to step in the middle to stop an oncoming attack of the devil. When you pray, you are asking God to intervene by stepping in the middle to stop the forward movement of the enemy. Divine intervention can be God *causing* something to happen or God *preventing* something from happening. At some point in your life you will need God to step in the middle to stop something or to make something happen for you.

Without prayer you are an open target for the devil. Without prayer you do not have a wall of defense around you. Now you can understand why Nehemiah wept over the broken walls of Jerusalem. The broken walls signified there was no defense and that the enemies of Israel had free access to attack the children of Israel. However a solid wall was a sign of a stronghold. This is why Jericho is referred to as a stronghold. You need to raise up a strong wall of prayer around your life to protect your coming in and going out. Without prayer there can be no intervention. Without prayer you are defenseless before the devil. As Nehemiah wept over the broken walls of Jerusalem, those who have no prayer walls will see tears of misery and pain.

When you pray, you are legally asking a Higher Superpower to intervene in your affairs

The realization that prayer is making intervention should motivate you to pray in order for God to intervene in your affairs. The prayer that God cannot answer is the prayer that you do not pray. If you want God to intervene then it is imperative that you lift your voice in prayer. When the early church was under attack from Herod, who had decapitated James the brother of John, God intervened when the church offered up prayers unceasingly. If the church had not prayed and asked God to intervene then Peter would have experienced the same fate that James had:

> *And he killed James the brother of John with the sword. And because he saw it pleased the Jews, he proceeded further to take Peter also. (Then were the days of unleavened bread.) And when he had apprehended him, he put him in prison, and delivered him to four quaternions of soldiers to keep him; intending after Easter to bring him forth to the people. Peter therefore was kept in prison: but prayer was made without ceasing of the church unto God for him.*
>
> ACTS 12:2-5

Satan can only proceed further when the church is silent in prayer. A prayer-less church gives Satan unrestrained access to steal, kill and destroy but you raise a wall of defense around you when you pray. Paul asked for prayer for a specific reason:

Finally, brethren, pray for us, that the word of the Lord may have free course, and be glorified, even as it is with you: And that we may be delivered from unreasonable and wicked men:

2 THESSALONIANS 3:1-2

Pray for God to intervene in order to be delivered from wicked men. Herod was a wicked man. Pharaoh was a wicked man and it took divine intervention through prayer to be delivered from the hands of these wicked men. You understand today there is no lack of wicked men and women in the earth that would seek to do harm to the church. We have to use the same weapon that the early church used to be delivered.

Daniel was thrown into the lion's den because of his prayer life and it was because of his prayer life that God intervened and sent an angel to shut the mouths of the hungry lions. Now that is what you call divine intervention.

God does nothing except in response to believing prayer – John Wesley

One of the greatest stories of divine intervention that you could read in the Old Testament is when King Hezekiah was sent a message of doom and disrespect. King Sennacherib of Assyria had been marching against all the fortified cities of Judah and had captured them. He then sent Rabshakeh to Jerusalem with a great army to deliver a message to King Hezekiah. Rabshakeh went and stood at the conduit of the upper pool, which is located on the road to the field where they washed and dried their clothes. Three men went to meet him and they were Eliakim son of Hilkiah, the palace supervisor, accompanied by Shebna the scribe and Joah son of Asaph, the secretary. Hear the message he gave to them:

The chief adviser said to them, "Tell Hezekiah: This is what the great king, the king of Assyria, says: 'What is your source of confidence? Your claim to have a strategy and military strength is just empty talk. In whom

*are you trusting, that you would dare to rebel against me? Look, you
must be trusting in Egypt, that splintered reed staff. If someone leans
on it for support, it punctures his hand and wounds him. That is what
Pharaoh king of Egypt does to all who trust in him! Perhaps you will tell
me, We are trusting in the Lord our God. But Hezekiah is the one who
eliminated his high places and altars and then told the people of Judah
and Jerusalem, You must worship at this altar. Now make a deal with
my master the king of Assyria, and I will give you two thousand horses,
provided you can find enough riders for them. Certainly you will not
refuse one of my master's minor officials and trust in Egypt for chariots
and horsemen. Furthermore it was by the command of the Lord that I
marched up against this land to destroy it. The Lord told me, March up
against this land and destroy it!'"*

ISAIAH 36:4-10 NET

Rabshakeh completely destroyed their confidence in God and in Hezekiah.
In fact he planted more seeds of doubt when he told them that God told him
to destroy their city. The three men then tried to reason with him to only
speak to them. See how Rabshakeh reacted:

But Rabshakeh said, **Hath my master sent me to thy master and to thee
to speak these words? hath he not sent me to the men that sit upon the
wall, that they may eat their own dung, and drink their own piss with you?**
*Then Rabshakeh stood, and cried with a loud voice in the Jews' language,
and said, Hear ye the words of the great king, the king of Assyria. Thus
saith the king, Let not Hezekiah deceive you: for he shall not be able to
deliver you. Neither let Hezekiah make you trust in the Lord, saying, The
Lord will surely deliver us: this city shall not be delivered into the hand
of the king of Assyria. Hearken not to Hezekiah: for thus saith the king
of Assyria, Make an agreement with me by a present, and come out to
me: and eat ye every one of his vine, and every one of his fig tree, and
drink ye every one the waters of his own cistern; Until I come and take
you away to a land like your own land, a land of corn and wine, a land*

of bread and vineyards. Beware lest Hezekiah persuade you, saying, The Lord will deliver us. Hath any of the gods of the nations delivered his land out of the hand of the king of Assyria? Where are the gods of Hamath and Arphad? where are the gods of Sepharvaim? and have they delivered Samaria out of my hand? Who are they among all the gods of these lands, that have delivered their land out of my hand, that the Lord should deliver Jerusalem out of my hand? But they held their peace, and answered him not a word: for the king's commandment was, saying, Answer him not. Then came Eliakim, the son of Hilkiah, that was over the household, and Shebna the scribe, and Joah, the son of Asaph, the recorder, to Hezekiah with their clothes rent, and told him the words of Rabshakeh.

ISAIAH 36:13-22

Rabshakeh was ruthless and totally disrespectful. In effect he was saying the people on the wall will be eating their own excrement and drinking their own urine once Sennacherib is done with them. The future looked bleak for Hezekiah and his nation. Rabshakeh went through the history of war successes that Sennacherib had and how no gods could deliver them from his hands. Rabshakeh boldly proclaimed that the same fate awaited Hezekiah and his people. What did Hezekiah do? When King Hezekiah heard this, he tore his clothes, put on sackcloth, and went to the Lord's temple and when he received letters from Sennacherib, this is what he did:

And Hezekiah received the letter from the hand of the messengers, and read it: and Hezekiah went up unto the house of the Lord, and spread it before the Lord. And Hezekiah prayed unto the Lord...

ISAIAH 37:14-15

Hezekiah spread the letters before God and began to pray asking God for divine intervention. The great prophet Isaiah then gave a prophetic word which released the angel of the Lord to wreak havoc against the King of Assyria: *'Then the angel of the Lord went forth, and smote in the camp of the Assyrians a hundred and fourscore and five thousand: and when they arose early in the morning, behold, they were all dead corpses'* (Isaiah 37:36). What was the end result?

> *Then the angel of the Lord went forth, and smote in the camp of the Assyrians a hundred and fourscore and five thousand: and when they arose early in the morning, behold, they were all dead corpses. So Sennacherib king of Assyria departed, and went and returned, and dwelt at Nineveh. And it came to pass, as he was worshipping in the house of Nisroch his god, that Adrammelech and Sharezer his sons smote him with the sword; and they escaped into the land of Armenia: and Esar–haddon his son reigned in his stead.*
>
> ISAIAH 37:38

Prayer is divine intervention to bring in divine justice. In a later chapter that looks at the depths and dimensions in prayer, we will give a thorough look at judicial prayer.

Prayer bends the omnipotence of heaven to your desire.
Prayer moves the hand that moves the world
– Charles Haddon Spurgeon

CHAPTER 5
SEVEN DIFFERENT FACETS OF PRAYER PART 1

As we start to delve into the different depths and dimensions in prayer, we want to look at seven different aspects of prayer in order for us to grasp what prayer is all about. Unfortunately people think all prayers are the same but nothing could be further from the truth. I am sure you have heard people say, 'Well, prayer is prayer.' Those who speak like that are only portraying their ignorance on this marvelous privilege. These seven aspects will give you a well rounded perspective of prayer which you can apply to your life's situations. I want you to imagine a golfer that has different types of clubs that he can choose, depending on the types of shots he needs to make. The purpose of having multiple clubs is to provide a range of distances and a choice of trajectories (higher or lower), governed by the different loft or angle on the face of each club. In the same way we are going to look into our prayer bag and pull out the appropriate prayer club in order for us to hit the right shot and continue on the right trajectory on our prayer course.

1 PRAYER IS RELATIONAL

"And he said unto them, When ye pray, say, Our Father which art in heaven, Hallowed be thy name. Thy kingdom come. Thy will be done, as in heaven, so in earth."

LUKE 11:2

The first thing I want you to grasp about prayer is that it is *the enhancing and deepening of your relationship with God*. Prayer is relational and communal; it is romancing God, taking your relationship to the next level. It is through prayer that we experience '*deep calleth unto deep*' (Psalm 42:7). When asked by his disciple, '*Lord, teach us to pray*' (Luke 11:1), Jesus responded, '*When ye pray, say, Our Father who art in heaven*' (Luke 11:2).

Jesus revealed to us that we acknowledge and connect with God through prayer. Through prayer you reveal your desire and pursuit for God:

I love them that love me; and those that seek me early shall find me.

PROVERBS 8:17

Then shall ye call upon me, and ye shall go and pray unto me, and I will hearken unto you. And ye shall seek me, and find me, when ye shall search for me with all your heart.

JEREMIAH 29:12-13

As I have said before, it is through prayer that you experientially understand the fatherhood of God, the high priesthood of Jesus and the comfort of the Holy Ghost. It is one thing to say, 'God is our father' and another to know Him as a *daddy*. Paul described this phenomenon in his epistle:

For ye have not received the spirit of bondage again to fear; but ye have received the Spirit of adoption, whereby we cry, Abba, Father.

ROMANS 8:15

And because ye are sons, God hath sent forth the Spirit of his Son into your hearts, crying, Abba, Father.

GALATIANS 4:6

I understand that God is the father of all spirits and all creation, but to me he is my Abba daddy; I run to Him for everything. There is a very important aspect of prayer as relational that we need to discuss. Some people think that they have to constantly shout when they are praying. While there is nothing wrong with some volume and intensity in your prayer, relating to your Heavenly Father should be as natural as relating to your friend, earthly parent or spouse. Ladies, how would you feel if every time you see you spouse, he screams, 'I LOVE YOU, I LOVE YOU, I REALLY REALLY DO!'? You would think your spouse is crazy and needs to be put in a straight jacket.

So while you can be intense, there is really no need to scream at God when you are being relational towards Him. It is through relational prayer that you will discover God as your Father, Jesus as your redeemer and the Holy Spirit as your Comforter. Remember, relationship is the ground for intimacy. Time investment fosters intimacy. The tripod upon which intimacy stands is *time*, *privacy* and *exclusivity*. If a believer wants to know God then it is imperative for him to have a relationship with prayer and a strong relationship with the Word. You can only be relational with God through His Word and prayer. This is how you get to know Him.

> *It is through prayer that you experientially understand the fatherhood of God, the high priesthood of Jesus and the comfort of the Holy Ghost*

2 PRAYER IS RESULT OBTAINING

The whole point of prayer is to obtain results. It is the means through which we appropriate Bible promises making dreams becoming realities. The reason people do not pray is because they do not know how to obtain results in prayer. However if results were materializing quickly, prayer would not be a chore that believers hate to do. Here are seven amazing words from the mouth of James, the Lord's brother:

Ye have not, because ye ask not

JAMES 4:2

These seven words are the answer to the manifold questions in the life of any believer. It points to where the problem is and puts a cap on all complaints. Here are a few questions and James' ultimate answer:

Q. Why don't I have a house?

A. Ye have not, because ye ask not.

Q. Why don't I have a stronger anointing?

A. Ye have not, because ye ask not.

Q. Why isn't my church growing?

A. Ye have not, because ye ask not.

Q. Why am I not blessed financially?

A. Ye have not, because ye ask not.

Q. Why isn't my ministry more impactful?

A. Ye have not, because ye ask not.

Q. Why am I not seeing souls saved?

A. Ye have not, because ye ask not.

Q. Why am I so powerless?

A. Ye have not, because ye ask not.

Q. Why isn't anyone healed in my ministry?

A. Ye have not, because ye ask not.

Q. Why isn't my business growing?

A. Ye have not, because ye ask not.

Q. Why isn't my career taking off?

A. Ye have not, because ye ask not.

The whole point of prayer is to obtain results

These seven words can be answered by seven even more powerful words. Observe the words of the foundational apostles in the early church:

...we will give ourselves continually to prayer...

ACTS 6:4

Prayer is result-obtaining. Look at a few things Jesus and the Scriptures said about prayer. Meditate upon them and let them saturate your spirit and your mind in order for them to manifest in your life.

Hitherto have ye asked nothing in my name: ask, and ye shall receive, that your joy may be full.

JOHN 16:24

Therefore I say unto you, What things soever ye desire, when ye pray, believe that ye receive them, and ye shall have them

MARK 11:24

Ask, and it shall be given you; seek, and ye shall find; knock, and it shall be opened unto you: 8 For every one that asketh receiveth; and he that seeketh findeth; and to him that knocketh it shall be opened. 9 Or what man is there of you, whom if his son ask bread, will he give him a stone? 10 Or if he ask a fish, will he give him a serpent?11 If ye then, being evil, know how to give good gifts unto your children, how much more shall your Father which is in heaven give good things to them that ask him?

MATTHEW 7:7-11

And all things, whatsoever ye shall ask in prayer, believing, ye shall receive.

MATTHEW 21:22

Ask of me, and I shall give thee the heathen for thine inheritance, and the uttermost parts of the earth for thy possession

PSALM 2:8

Ask ye of the Lord rain in the time of the latter rain; so the Lord shall make bright clouds, and give them showers of rain, to every one grass in the field.

ZECHARIAH 10:1

It is through prayer that we appropriate Bible promises, taking them from the pages of a book and from the realm of the spirit enabling us to physically experience them. This is how prayer obtains Bible results.

Remember relationship is the ground for intimacy and time investment fosters intimacy

3 PRAYER IS RESTORING AND REVERSING THE COURSE OF NATURE AND LIFE'S EVENTS.

The Bible is filled with examples of how, through prayer the course of nature was reversed. Through the reversal and restoring power of prayer, you will find yourself in your desired haven or destiny.

Then they cry unto the Lord in their trouble, and he bringeth them out of their distresses. He maketh the storm a calm, so that the waves thereof are still. Then are they glad because they be quiet; so he bringeth them unto their desired haven.

PSALM 107:28-30

Prayer has power over life's circumstances. It has power over the course of nature, to either reverse or accelerate it. When prayer unites with the purposes of God, it lays itself out to secure those purposes.

Abraham, the covenant friend of God, was a glowing illustration of one of the Old Testament patriarchs who strongly believed in prayer, knowing its power over the course of nature. In studying Abraham's life we discover that after his calling, he set to go out into an unknown country. During this journey with his family and household servants, whenever he came to a stop for the night, or longer, he would always erect an altar, and '*called upon the name of the Lord.*' An altar is a place where the natural connects with the Supernatural. Abraham always desired to connect with God. These altars had a dual purpose, a place where he would call upon God personally and where his family and descendants could also call upon God. Abraham was a strong believer in prayer and one of the greatest intercessors in the Old Testament. Many know Abraham as the father of faith and he earned this title through prayer. There is no conflict between faith and prayer. Prayer is an expression of your faith and your faith is released through prayer. You need to grasp that. As faith teachers we have often said that faith is released by words. This is true but even more so in prayer. Abraham, the father of faith was a man of prayer.

〉 Abimelech and Abraham

God Himself testified that Abraham was a man of prayer. When Abraham encountered King Abimelech, the latter took Sarah into his harem. However God spared him from judgment because of his personal integrity and revealed to him in a dream that Sarah was the wife of Abraham:.

> *Now therefore restore the man his wife; for he is a prophet, and **he shall pray for thee**, and thou shalt live: and if thou restore her not, know thou that thou shalt surely die, thou, and all that are thine.*
>
> GENESIS 20:7

Notice the power that Abraham had in prayer. His prayer had the power to prolong the life of King Abimelech. Evidently Abimelech was sick but there was also another issue in his kingdom: all the women in his family were barren due to him taking Sarah in his harem:

> *So **Abraham prayed unto God: and God healed** Abimelech, and his wife, and his maidservants; and they bare children. For the Lord had fast closed up all the wombs of the house of Abimelech, because of Sarah Abraham's wife.*
>
> GENESIS 20:17-18

Through Abraham's prayer, Abimelech was healed and God also restored the fruitfulness of the women in his family. Prayer reverses, restores, rejuvenates and revitalizes the cycle of nature. Abraham and Sarah were old and medically speaking were beyond their capacity to produce a child, yet through faith and prayer, nature was reversed and a promised seed was born in Isaac.

The Bible is filled with examples of how, through prayer the course of nature was reversed

⟩ Israel's Deliverance from Egypt

Israel found themselves under the evil hand of the wicked Pharaoh who had planned their destruction. Their existence under Pharaoh's administration was bitter and rigorous. The children of God needed deliverance. How were they delivered?

> *When Jacob was come into Egypt, and **your fathers cried unto the Lord, then the Lord sent Moses** and Aaron, which brought forth your fathers out of Egypt, and made them dwell in this place*
>
> 1 SAMUEL 12:8

> *And it came to pass in process of time, that the king of Egypt died: and the children of Israel sighed by reason of the bondage, and they cried, and their cry came up unto God by reason of the bondage. And God heard their groaning, and God remembered his covenant with Abraham, with Isaac, and with Jacob.*
>
> EXODUS 2:23-24

Their deliverance began with praying. The genesis of the exodus was due to the praying of the people. Prayer preceded the emancipation. That is always the case. Prayer precedes victory.

⟩ Moses

Israel, as a nation would have met their just destruction and their just fate – after their apostate worship of the golden calf – if it had it not been for the intercession, interposition and unrelenting and importunate prayer of Moses for forty days' and forty nights!

> *And the Lord said unto Moses, I have seen this people, and, behold, it is a stiffnecked people: Now therefore let me alone, that my wrath may wax hot against them, and that I may consume them: and I will make of thee a great nation. And Moses besought the Lord his God, and said, Lord, why doth thy wrath wax hot against thy people, which thou hast brought forth out of the land of Egypt with great power, and with a mighty hand? Wherefore should the Egyptians speak, and say, For mischief did he bring them out, to slay them in the mountains, and to consume them from the face of the earth? Turn from thy fierce wrath, and repent of this evil against thy people. Remember Abraham, Isaac, and Israel, thy servants, to whom thou swarest by thine own self, and saidst unto them, I will multiply your seed as the stars of heaven, and all this land that I have spoken of will I give unto your seed, and they shall inherit it for ever. And the Lord repented of the evil which he thought to do unto his people.*
>
> EXODUS 32:9-14

Judgment was pronounced over Israel after their great sin, yet through prayer, Moses halted it. He stayed before God in intercession and pleaded his case efficiently so that God relented from what He purposed to do. This is the power in prayer and the power of prayer.

The genesis of the exodus was due to the praying of the people

> **Leprosy of Miram and her healing**

Another interesting event that reveals how prayer reverses and restores is the case of Miriam who contracted leprosy:

> *And Miriam and Aaron spake against Moses because of the Ethiopian woman whom he had married: for he had married an Ethiopian woman.*

*And they said, Hath the Lord indeed spoken only by Moses? hath he not spoken also by us? And the Lord heard it. (Now the man Moses was very meek, above all the men which were upon the face of the earth.) And the Lord spake suddenly unto Moses, and unto Aaron, and unto Miriam, Come out ye three unto the tabernacle of the congregation. And they three came out. And the Lord came down in the pillar of the cloud, and stood in the door of the tabernacle, and called Aaron and Miriam: and they both came forth...And the anger of the Lord was kindled against them; and he departed. And the cloud departed from off the tabernacle; and, behold, Miriam became leprous, white as snow: and Aaron looked upon Miriam, and, behold, she was leprous. And Aaron said unto Moses, Alas, my lord, I beseech thee, lay not the sin upon us, wherein we have done foolishly, and wherein we have sinned. Let her not be as one dead, of whom the flesh is half consumed when he cometh out of his mother's womb. **And Moses cried unto the Lord, saying, Heal her now, O God, I beseech thee.** And the Lord said unto Moses, If her father had but spit in her face, should she not be ashamed seven days? let her be shut out from the camp seven days, and after that let her be received in again. And Miriam was shut out from the camp seven days: and the people journeyed not till Miriam was brought in again.*

NUMBERS 12:1-5; 9-15

It was the prayer of Moses that reversed the curse of leprosy upon Miriam. When you pray, things will be reversed and restored back into your life.

4 PRAYER IS THE RELEASING OF RESOURCES

When you pray, resources are released, enabling you to fulfill your life's calling and destiny. The apostle Paul taught us to pray so that we come behind in no gift:

I thank my God always on your behalf, for the grace of God which is given you by Jesus Christ; That in every thing ye are enriched by him, in all utterance, and in all knowledge; Even as the testimony of Christ was confirmed in you: So that ye come behind in no gift; waiting for the coming of our Lord Jesus Christ:

1 CORINTHIANS 1:4-7

We must not allow ourselves to come behind when the mighty weapon of prayer is at our disposal. We see the connection between releasing of resources and prayer all over the Bible. We see it both in the Old Testament and the New Testament. Here are a few examples:

〉 Nehemiah and the wall

Then the king said unto me, For what dost thou make request? So I prayed to the God of heaven. And I said unto the king, If it please the king, and if thy servant have found favour in thy sight, that thou wouldest send me unto Judah, unto the city of my fathers' sepulchres, that I may build it. And the king said unto me, (the queen also sitting by him) For how long shall thy journey be? and when wilt thou return? So it pleased the king to send me; and I set him a time. Moreover I said unto the king, If it please the king, let letters be given me to the governors beyond the river, that they may convey me over till I come into Judah; And a letter unto Asaph the keeper of the king's forest, that he may give me timber to make beams for the gates of the palace which appertained to the house, and for the wall of the city, and for the house that I shall enter into. And the king granted me, according to the good hand of my God upon me.

NEHEMIAH 2:4-8

〉 Jesus's feeding of the 5,000

And he commanded the multitude to sit down on the grass, and took the five loaves, and the two fishes, and looking up to heaven, he blessed, and brake, and gave the loaves to his disciples, and the disciples to the multitude. And they did all eat, and were filled: and they took up of the fragments that remained twelve baskets full. And they that had eaten were about five thousand men, beside women and children.

MATTHEW 14:19-21

⟩ Miracles, Signs and Wonders

In Acts 4:30 the church asked in prayer, '*Stretch out your hand to heal and perform miraculous signs and wonders through the name of your holy servant Jesus.*' We see this answer in the following chapter:

> *And by the hands of the apostles were many signs and wonders wrought among the people; and they were all with one accord in Solomon's porch*
>
> ACTS 5:12

⟩ Workers and harvesters

> *Therefore said he unto them, The harvest truly is great, but the labourers are few: pray ye therefore the Lord of the harvest, that he would send forth labourers into his harvest.*
>
> LUKE 10:2

When you pray, the resources that you need will be released. God wants us to be fruitful in every good work and there is a connection between prayer and fruitfulness. When Hannah was fruitless, she became fruitful through prayer. The same thing happened for Elizabeth and Zacharias who were fruitless in their old age but as Zacharias offered incense in the temple, which is symbolic of prayer, their long stretch of fruitlessness was turned into fruitfulness through the birth of John the Baptist.

> ## Prayer is the key to prosperity

Prayer will turn a long stretch of fruitlessness into fruitfulness

CHAPTER 6
SEVEN DIFFERENT FACETS OF PRAYER PART 2

WE have been busy looking at the different facets or aspects of prayer in order for us to have a healthy understanding of our subject. Prayer is only boring for those who do not understand its manifold dimensions. Understanding these aspects of prayer will enable you to wield this weapon as a skilled professional who does so in their chosen field towards the desired results. Let us proceed to the fifth facet.

5 PRAYER IS THE RENDING AND RENTING OF THE HEAVENS

If only you would split open the heavens and come down! The mountains would quake at your presence.

GOD'S WORD® TRANSLATION

And I will break the pride of your power; and I will make your heaven as iron, and your earth as brass: And your strength shall be spent in vain: for your land shall not yield her increase, neither shall the trees of the land yield their fruits.

LEVITICUS 26:19-20

Isaiah's great cry was, '*Oh that thou wouldest rend the heavens, that thou wouldest come down, that the mountains might flow down at thy presence...*' (Isaiah 64:1). An open heaven is a must if you want to live a life of blessings and prosperity. The opposite to this is a closed heaven, which is hard living:

And thy heaven that is over thy head shall be brass, and the earth that is under thee shall be iron.

DEUTERONOMY 28:23

A brass heaven results in an iron earth where nothing grows and everything becomes hard. This is why it is imperative for you to live and operate under an open heaven. Even the Lord Jesus did not do anything, did not minister, did not preach, did no miracles until the heaven was opened.

> *Now when all the people were baptized, it came to pass, that **Jesus also being baptized, and praying, the heaven was opened, And the Holy Ghost descended in a bodily** shape like a dove upon him, and a voice came from heaven, which said, Thou art my beloved Son; in thee I am well please.*
>
> LUKE 3:21-22

I want you to understand that good things happen when the heavens are opened and bad things happen when the heavens are closed. In the next chapter I will show you in more detail the importance of an opened heaven.

6 PRAYER IS REVIVING AND REPLENISHING

Prayer brings revival and a replenishing. All through the Scriptures we can see that. Look at the 10-day prayer meeting in the upper room in Acts:

> *And when they were come in, they went up into an upper room, where abode both Peter, and James, and John, and Andrew, Philip, and Thomas, Bartholomew, and Matthew, James the son of Alphaeus, and Simon Zelotes, and Judas the brother of James. These all continued with one accord in prayer and supplication, with the women, and Mary the mother of Jesus, and with his brethren*
>
> ACTS 1:13-14

Here are the end results:

> *And when the day of Pentecost was fully come, they were all with one accord in one place. And suddenly there came a sound from heaven as of a rushing mighty wind, and it filled all the house where they were sitting. And there appeared unto them cloven tongues like as of fire, and it sat upon each of them. And they were all filled with the Holy Ghost,*

and began to speak with other tongues, as the Spirit gave them utterance.

ACTS 2:1-4

Then they that gladly received his word were baptized: and the same day there were added unto them about three thousand souls. And they continued stedfastly in the apostles' doctrine and fellowship, and in breaking of bread, and in prayers. And fear came upon every soul: and many wonders and signs were done by the apostles.

ACTS 2:41-43

The early church had a strong prayer force:

And they, continuing daily with one accord in the temple, and breaking bread from house to house, did eat their meat with gladness and singleness of heart, Praising God, and having favour with all the people. And the Lord added to the church daily such as should be saved.

ACTS 2:46-47

The connection between prayer and revival is unmistakably clear. We see it through the Scriptures and through past and present generations. Prayer is the catalyst for revival. **It is not our eloquence of preaching that will bring a move of God but the rending of our hearts before the Lord.** May God give you and I the spirit of prayer like the believers of old who would hold on to the horns of the altar and pray through till they and the church were revived. The great South Korean revival was birthed through prayer. The Nigerian phenomenon of explosive church growth is due to people praying incessantly. When we lose our fervor for praying we lose the fires and favors of revival! Look anywhere in the world where a church is thriving in revival and you will see a strong prayer base.

Brethren, we shall never see much change for the better in our churches in general till the prayer meeting occupies a higher place in the esteem of Christians – Charles Haddon Spurgeon

---

7 PRAYER IS RESISTANCE AND REIGNING IN WARFARE

If you think that prayer is only relational and not confrontational then you are mistaken. There are three main stratums of prayer:

❖ Communion = relationship and fellowship.

❖ Petition = needs and desires.

❖ Intercession = warfare.

Prayer is not just communing with and asking God for things. Prayer is also warfare. *Prayer is conflict for conquest*. It is undeniable that spiritual warfare is real because we have an enemy in Satan and his wicked hosts (Ephesians 6:12) and this is why we are told to put on the whole armor of God in order to pray and win the battle. We pray to establish the will, the plans and purposes of God. This is the realm of the clash of powers. This is the realm where you join Jesus, the Holy Spirit, Moses, Abraham, Samuel, Jacob, Daniel and Elijah, Paul and Epaphras. There are rules of engagement when entering in to prayer in order to obtain the results that we are looking for. Prayer is tapping into divine strategies for fellowship, fighting and furtherance of life and ministry

------

We pray to establish the will, the plans and purposes of God. This is the realm of the clash of powers

This is why there are different types of prayers:

* Prayer of Petition.
* Prayer of Supplication.
* Prayer of binding and loosing.
* Prayer of agreement.
* Prayer of consecration.
* Prayer of intercession.
* Prayer of faith.
* Prayer of importunity.
* Praying in the Spirit.
* Praying with the Spirit.

You can engage different prayers for different situations. Engaging prayer as resistance to the enemy's plans is necessary for us to live in peace and victory. Now let us have an in depth look at rending the heavens through prayer.

Prayer is tapping into divine strategies for fellowship, fighting and furtherance of life and ministry

CHAPTER 7
PRAYER IS THE RENDING AND OPENING OF THE HEAVENS PART 1

THIS is a very important aspect in the development of your prayer life and of course we will glean from the prayer life of Jesus. Prayer is the opening and the rending of the heavens. Without the heavens being opened, Jesus did nothing of significance! He did not preach his first sermon, heal the sick, cast out devils or launch His ministry until the heavens were opened unto Him. He did not attempt to fulfill destiny without an opened heaven. This dimension of prayer – that you must understand – is its offensive side. If you only think that prayer is relational, communal and petitional with God then you are doing yourself a gross injustice. Of course those are great facets to familiarize yourself with but you also need to understand that *prayer is warfare*. Now I am going to go through the synoptic Gospels and look at this monumental event in the life of Jesus and I want you to pay very close attention to the words *heavens* and *heaven*. As you know, one would be plural and the other singular.

*Then cometh Jesus from Galilee to Jordan unto John, to be baptized of him. But John forbad him, saying, I have need to be baptized of thee, and comest thou to me? And Jesus answering said unto him, Suffer it to be so now: for thus it becometh us to fulfil all righteousness. Then he suffered him. And Jesus, when he was baptized, went up straightway out of the water: **and, lo, the heavens were opened unto him**, and he saw the Spirit of God descending like a dove, and lighting upon him: **And lo a voice from heaven**, saying, This is my beloved Son, in whom I am well pleased.*
MATTHEW 3:13-17

And it came to pass in those days, that Jesus came from Nazareth of Galilee, and was baptized of John in Jordan. And straightway coming up *out of the water, **he saw the heavens opened,** and the Spirit like a dove descending upon him: **And there came a voice from heaven,** saying, Thou art my beloved Son, in whom I am well pleased.*

MARK 1:9-11

Jesus did not preach his first sermon, heal the sick, cast out devils or launch His ministry until the heavens were opened unto Him

---

*Now when all the people were baptized, it came to pass, that Jesus also being baptized, and praying, **the heaven was opened,** And the Holy Ghost descended in a bodily shape like a dove upon him, and a voice came from **heaven,** which said, Thou art my beloved Son; in thee I am well pleased.*

LUKE 3:21-22

*And I knew him not: but that he should be made manifest to Israel, therefore am I come baptizing with water. And John bare record, saying, **I saw the Spirit descending from heaven like a dove, and it abode upon him.** And I knew him not: but he that sent me to baptize with water, the same said unto me, Upon whom thou shalt see the Spirit descending, and remaining on him, the same is he which baptizeth with the Holy Ghost.*

JOHN 1:31-33

As you can see there is a recurring pattern of the words *heavens* and *heaven.* Let me give you two more examples from the life of Stephen and the book of Hebrews:

*But he, being full of the Holy Ghost, **looked up stedfastly into heaven, and saw the glory of God, and Jesus standing on the right hand of God,** And said, Behold, **I see the heavens opened,** and the Son of man standing on the right hand of God.*

ACTS 7:55-56

Seeing then that we have a great high priest, that is passed into the heavens, Jesus the Son of God, let us hold fast our profession.

HEBREWS 4:14

When the heavens were opened, Stephen saw beyond the air space – the firmament – and saw into the very Throne Room of God where Jesus was standing at the right and of the Father. Isaiah's great plea was for God to split the heavens:

Oh that thou wouldest rend the heavens, that thou wouldest come down, that the mountains might flow down at thy presence, As when the melting fire burneth, the fire causeth the waters to boil, to make thy name known to thine adversaries, that the nations may tremble at thy presence! When thou didst terrible things which we looked not for, thou camest down, the mountains flowed down at thy presence.

ISAIAH 64:1-3

If only you would split open the heavens and come down! The mountains would quake at your presence.

GOD'S WORD® TRANSLATION

Can you hear Isaiah's heartfelt and fervent intercessory cry to God? Every believer, just like Jesus, must endeavor to live and operate under an open heaven and every believer must have the same urgency of fervency in prayer to call for the rending of the heavens, just like Isaiah. Remember that Isaiah encountered God (as he revealed earlier in his book, Isaiah 6:1-9). When Uzziah the king died, Isaiah saw the Lord sitting on His throne, high and exalted, and His robe filled the whole temple with seraphims around Him crying out, '*Holy, holy, holy, is the Lord of hosts: the whole earth is full of his glory*' (Isaiah 6:3). When God was in the temple, the earth was filled with His glory. This is why Isaiah was making a plea for Him to come down so the earth could be filled with the glory, which is literally the heaviness of His presence.

Now when I say, '*Prayer is the rending or renting of the heavens*', I am not referring to the third heaven: the place of God's abode and where the throne of grace is – that heaven is not on lock-down. I am referring to the second heaven – also known as the heavenlies – where principalities, powers and demons are.

> Defining the first, second and third heavens

We have already seen from the Synoptic Gospels and Acts that the Bible talks about the heavens and heaven. Paul talks about the third heaven. Moses tells us in Genesis, '*In the beginning God created the heaven and the earth*' (Genesis 1:1). Your Authorized Version says 'heaven' but in Hebrew it is the word *shamayim* which is a plural form meaning 'heavens and heights.' As a matter of fact most Bible translations employ the word 'heavens'. We see the proper use of the word in the second chapter of Genesis: '*Thus the heavens and the earth were finished, and all the host of them*' (Genesis 2:1). Paul penned these words in his second epistle to the Corinthians:

> *I knew a man in Christ above fourteen years ago, (whether in the body, I cannot tell; or whether out of the body, I cannot tell: God knoweth;) such an one caught up to the third heaven. And I knew such a man, (whether in the body, or out of the body, I cannot tell: God knoweth;) How that he was caught up into paradise, and heard unspeakable words, which it is not lawful for a man to utter.*
>
> 2 CORINTHIANS 12:2-4

What specifically is the 'third heaven'? First of all, if there is a third heaven then we can safely conclude that there is a first and second. The author of Hebrews unveiled that Jesus went through the heavens (Hebrews 4:14) and Bible scholars agree that the third heaven is God's abode of dominion. Traditionally here is how scholars have defined the three heavens:

* Heaven where God is, also known as the third heaven.
* The stella heaven, where the stars and planets are, the universe, also known as the second heaven.

❖ The atmosphere above us which is also known as the firmament being the first heaven.

That is just fine! However we want to look beyond tradition because Paul also engaged the word 'heavenlies' and 'high places' in Ephesians:

For we wrestle not against flesh and blood, but against principalities, against powers, against the rulers of the darkness of this world, against spiritual wickedness in high places.

EPHESIANS 6:12

For our struggle is not against flesh and blood, but against the rulers, against the powers, against the world rulers of this darkness, against the spiritual forces of evil in the heavens.

N.E.T

With Paul's use of the word heavens or heavenlies, we have to define where this struggle is taking place. There cannot be a fourth heaven because Paul already said there was three. So here is a more updated understanding of the three heavens:

❖ **The first heaven** is what Genesis calls the atmospheric heaven, the physical heavens of the sky, with stars, sun and moon which our eyes can see and the outer space containing planets.

❖ **The second heaven or middle heaven** is the operating room of the adversary and what Paul calls 'the heavenly places' in Ephesians. This is an unseen spiritual sphere above and around us where unseen forces, both demonic and angelic are at work. John the Revelator says, '*And I saw another angel fly in the midst of heaven, having the everlasting gospel to preach unto them that dwell on the earth, and to every nation, and kindred, and tongue, and people*' (Revelation 14:6). The word *midst* is the Greek word *mesooranaymay* meaning 'middle'. This is the realm of angelic forces and demonic forces activities and battles. This is the real Star Wars. This unseen but nonetheless real world has direct impact and implications on the natural seen world.

❖ **The third heaven** is the one that Paul was caught up into, the highest heaven – God's dwelling place. This is where the throne room is, this is where Jesus is right now and where the believer goes after death.

❭ What do we mean?

What do we mean when we say prayer is the rending of the heavens? It is about shifting things in the heavenlies, in the second heaven in order for things to be right on the earth. Isaiah reveals to us that when the heaven is rended, God comes down and His presence manifests. You see the things of the heavenlies have direct impact upon the natural state that we see. Many people try to change the natural from the natural but this is nothing more than futile labor. The rending, or the opening of the heavens is shifting things in the spirit to have a positive impact upon your earthly domain. There is a direct correlation with what is going on in the heavenlies and what is happening in the earth. There is a direct impact!

The Lord shall open unto thee his good treasure, the heaven to give the rain unto thy land in his season, and to bless all the work of thine hand:
DEUTERONOMY 28:12

And thy heaven that is over thy head shall be brass, and the earth that is under thee shall be iron.
DEUTERONOMY 28:23

In a nutshell, here is what you need to grasp:

❖ Bad things happen when the heavens are closed.
❖ Good things happen when the heavens are opened.
❖ A closed heaven is a curse.
❖ An opened heaven is a blessing.

A brass heaven results in an iron earth, meaning a hard life and bondage. In the Bible, brass speaks of judgment, suffering and fetters (Judges 16:21, Numbers 21:9, John 3:14). As you can see from the above Scripture a brass heaven or a closed heaven results in hardship and non-productivity on the earth. Here are 25 manifestations of a closed and brass heaven in Israel of old:

1. Drought and famine.
2. Poverty, debt and lack.
3. Dispersion.
4. Barrenness.
5. Bondages.
6. Stagnancy.
7. Captivity.
8. Subject to the enemy.
9. Untimely death.
10. Curses.
11. Unyielding ground no matter how much planting.
12. Fruitless labor.
13. Loss.
14. Pestilences.
15. Oppressions.
16. Bad marriages and rebellious families.
17. Recurring calamities and sicknesses.
18. Fear.
19. Miseries.
20. No revelation, no open vision and no voice of God.
21. No salvations resulting in an anti-God society.
22. Spiritual blindness.
23. Fruitless ministry.
24. Increase of sin, iniquity and wickedness.
25. A life of no joy, no harvest and no laughter resulting in Ichabod (the glory has departed).

And I will break the pride of your power; and I will make your heaven as iron, and your earth as brass: And your strength shall be spent in vain: for your land shall not yield her increase, neither shall the trees of the land yield their fruit

LEVITICUS 26:19-20

It is a bad situation when one is living under a closed and brass heaven. Not only does it affect us on a personal level but it also affects us on a national and ministerial level. Ministry is fruitless under a closed heaven. Many are frustrated in ministry because they do not see salvations or miracles. They are preaching hard, doing evangelism, praying for the sick and yet to no avail. Why?

*And in this mountain will the LORD of hosts make unto all peoples a feast of fat things, a feast of wines on the lees, of fat things full of marrow, of wines on the lees well refined. And He will destroy in this mountain the face of **the covering that is cast over all peoples, and the veil that is spread over all nations.***

ISAIAH 25:9

The rending or the opening of the heavens is shifting things in the spirit to have a positive impact upon your earthly domain

The reason we are not seeing the multitudes receiving salvation is because there is a veil that is spread over all the nation; there is a veil spread over your city holding the people in captivity. The different renditions of this verse from several translations will be an eye opener:

At that time he will remove the cloud of gloom, the pall of death that hangs over the earth.

THE LIVING BIBLE

*On this mountain he will swallow up the shroud that is over all the peoples,
the woven covering that is over all the nations;*

NET BIBLE

*And in this mountain he will put an end to the shade covering the face
of all peoples, and the veil which is stretched over all nations*

BIBLE IN BASIC ENGLISH

*On this mountain he will destroy the shroud that enfolds all peoples, the
sheet that covers all nations;*

N.I.V

*On this mountain he will remove the veil of grief covering all people and
the mask covering all nations.*

GOD'S WORD TRANSLATION

A closed heaven is a woven sheet of gloom that covers a person, a city
and a nation, stopping it from experiencing revival and breakthrough.
We cannot enjoy the feast of fat things when the heaven over us is brass.
However prayer is the rending of the closed and brass heaven. Things flow
under an open heaven, just as in Jacob's dream of an open heaven where
he saw angels ascending and descending; there are angelic activities and
a flow of the supernatural results.

---

*The reason why we are not seeing the multitudes receiving
salvations and revivals is because there is a veil
that is spread over all the nation*

Here's what I want you to believe to happen for you when the heavens are opened:

1. **Great events and great manifestations** take place when the heavens are opened. Great events will take place in your life when the heavens are opened. Even the Second Coming of Jesus to deal with His enemies will be because of an opened heaven:

   And I saw heaven opened, and behold a white horse; and he that sat upon him was called Faithful and True, and in righteousness he doth judge and make war.

   REVELATION 19:11

2. **The physical manifestation of the Spirit** occurs when the heaven is opened. You need the glory to manifest in your life and produce outstanding results to baffle the devil. Signs and wonders will be a reality through an opened heaven:

   Now when all the people were baptized, it came to pass, that Jesus also being baptized, and praying, the heaven was opened, And the Holy Ghost descended in a bodily shape like a dove upon him, and a voice came from heaven, which said, Thou art my beloved Son; in thee I am well please

   LUKE 3:21-22

3. **Dominion upon the earth** is connected to greatness in the heavens. Before we see things in the earth they are first manifested in the heavens. Influence, impact and authority are yours when you operate under an open heaven. This is not just for ministers but for whatever field you find yourself in; you are to dominate and be great:

   It is thou, O king, that art grown and become strong: for thy greatness is grown, and reacheth unto heaven, and thy dominion to the end of the earth.

   DANIEL 4:22

Here are some things that will occur when you live under an open heaven:

❖ Under an open heaven life will open up for you.

❖ Under an open heaven new opportunities will open up for you.

❖ Under an open heaven what others cannot do you will do.

❖ Under an open heaven life, ministry and destiny flows easier.

❖ Under an open heaven there are angelic activities for heirs of salvation.

❖ Under an open heaven there will be unity in the family.

❖ Under an open heaven prayers are answered.

❖ Under an open heaven fruitfulness will be the order of the day.

❖ Under an open heaven prosperity flows.

❖ Under an open heaven there will be promotion.

❖ Under an open heaven there will be no delay, only acceleration towards fulfillment of destiny.

❖ Under an open heaven there will be bountiful harvest.

❖ Under an open heaven you experience divine healing, divine health and divine life.

❖ Under an open heaven you will have longevity of life.

❖ Under an open heaven generational curses and your enemies will be crushed before you.

❖ Under an open heaven all demonic resistance is broken.

❖ Under an open heaven the devil becomes your victim but under a closed heaven you are the victim of the devil.

Under an open heaven, what others cannot do, you will do

Now let's look at the blessings of some in the Bible who lived under an open heaven.

CHAPTER 8
PRAYER IS THE RENDING AND OPENING OF THE HEAVENS PART 2

W E have been looking at the rending of the heavens as was the plea of Isaiah. We have discovered that a closed heaven is a curse and an open heaven is a blessing. As previously stated, Jesus did not do anything in ministry until the heavens were opened unto Him. He literally broke a four hundred-year sealed heaven to start His ministry. We know that between Malachi and Matthew there is a period of 400 years which theologians call the *silent period*. It is interesting to note that the very last word in the Old Testament is the word 'curse' (Malachi 4:6). Jesus broke that curse of 400 years silence and brought the glory into Israel. There are great blessings in living under an open heaven. We can see these clearly in the Bible. Here are a few examples:

§ Jesus

Now when all the people were baptized, it came to pass, that Jesus also being baptized, and praying, the heaven was opened, And the Holy Ghost descended in a bodily shape like a dove upon him, and a voice came from heaven, which said, Thou art my beloved Son; in thee I am well please.

LUKE 3:21-22

And straightway coming up out of the water, he saw the heavens opened, and the Spirit like a dove descending upon him:

MARK 1:10

The words, 'the heavens opened' as employed in Mark is *skhizo* in Greek, meaning 'to split and sever'. It is literally a violent renting. When Jesus prayed, the 400 years *silent period* was torn apart and the Holy Spirit descended upon Jesus, releasing Him into a supernatural ministry. So when we look at the life of Jesus, an open heaven resulted in four things:

❭ Manifestation of the Holy Spirit. The glory came down

Now when all the people were baptized, it came to pass, that Jesus also being baptized, and praying, the heaven was opened, And the Holy Ghost descended in a bodily shape like a dove upon him, and a voice came from heaven, which said, Thou art my beloved Son; in thee I am well please.

LUKE 3:21-22

❭ Access to the voice of God

...and a voice came from heaven, which said, Thou art my beloved Son; in thee I am well please.

LUKE 3:22

❭ The anointing for supernatural ministry

*And Jesus **returned in the power of the Spirit into Galilee:** and there went out a fame of him through all the region round about. And he taught in their synagogues, being glorified of all... And there was delivered unto him the book of the prophet Esaias. And when he had opened the book, he found the place where it was written, **The Spirit of the Lord is upon me, because he hath anointed me to preach the gospel to the poor; he hath sent me to heal the brokenhearted, to preach deliverance to the captives, and recovering of sight to the blind, to set at liberty them that are bruised, To preach the acceptable year of the Lord.***

LUKE 4:14, 15, 17-19

❭ Healings, deliverances and miracles

Now when the sun was setting, all they that had any sick with divers diseases brought them unto him; and he laid his hands on every one of them, and healed them.

LUKE 4:40

*And they bring unto him one that was deaf, and had an impediment in his speech; and they beseech him to put his hand upon him. And he took him aside from the multitude, and put his fingers into his ears, and he spit, and touched his tongue; And looking up to heaven, he sighed, and saith unto him, **Ephphatha, that is, Be opened**. And straightway his ears were opened, and the string of his tongue was loosed, and he spake plain.*

MARK 7:32-35

Can you see how there is a direct correlation between what goes on in the heavens and on the earth? Before the miracle took place on earth, Jesus looked into heaven.

⑤ Daniel

The prophet Daniel had to fast and pray for 21-days to break the canopy and hindrance of the Prince of Persia in the heavenlies for his answer to manifest:

In those days I Daniel was mourning three full weeks... Then said he unto me, Fear not, Daniel: for from the first day that thou didst set thine heart to understand, and to chasten thyself before thy God, thy words were heard, and I am come for thy words. But the prince of the kingdom of Persia withstood me one and twenty days: but, lo, Michael, one of the chief princes, came to help me; and I remained there with the kings of Persia.

DANIEL 10:2, 12-13

This is a very important lesson on prayer and the rending of the heavens. The verses from the book of Daniel teach about conflict in prayer and contending with the enemy in prayer. At the time the Prince of Persia was the principality over Persia. Although Persia had a physical ruling monarch in Cyrus, it was the principality behind the scenes that was pulling all the strings. The angel revealed to Daniel that from the first day that he prayed the answer was released but here was an obstruction that delayed his answer from manifesting. Here is how you need to see this:

Daniel prayed – God answered – Prince of Persia obstructed.

Earth called – Heaven answered – heavenlies obstructed.

First heaven called – Third heaven answered – Second heaven obstructed.

Even though there was resistance and opposition in the heavenlies, Daniel kept praying and there was a shift as Michael overthrew the Prince of Persia and hence the answer was delivered to Daniel. In the life of Daniel, an open heaven resulted in his answer manifesting and there was angelic activity.

*Persistency in prayer caused a shift
in the realm of the spirit*

Paul

Paul was a praying man. He travailed in the Spirit for the churches (Galatians 4:27) and for souls to be saved. Paul encountered opposition in the ministry just like all of us but he won the battle in the heavenlies. We can see what he says in regards to Ephesus:

If after the manner of men I have fought with beasts at Ephesus
                                                1 CORINTHIANS 15:32

The beasts of Ephesus were the ruling principalities over the region which manifested through ungodly and wicked people. Now don't put your eyes on the people but look beyond them to the spiritual entities that blinded and bound these people, using them as weapons of wickedness. Paul fought them. Now we know he did not fight physically. How did he do it?

For we wrestle not against flesh and blood, but against principalities, against powers, against the rulers of the darkness of this world, against spiritual wickedness in high places...Praying always with all prayer and supplication in the Spirit, and watching thereunto with all perseverance and supplication for all saints;

EPHESIANS 6:12, 18

His battles over Asia and Ephesus were done in prayers – in travailing and intercessory prayers to remove the covering clouds. Look at the outcome:

And this continued by the space of two years; so that all they which dwelt in Asia heard the word of the Lord Jesus, both Jews and Greeks. And God wrought special miracles by the hands of Paul: So that from his body were brought unto the sick handkerchiefs or aprons, and the diseases departed from them, and the evil spirits went out of them.

ACTS 19:10-12

You must understand that at that time, Ephesus was known as the 'Treasure house of Asia' and 'The Vanity Fair of Asia'. According to William Barclay's commentary, she was also the center of paganism, the Temple of Diana being the central figure. Ephesus was also famed for her charms and spells (called the 'Ephesian Letters') which supposedly brought a safe end to a journey, children to those who were barren and success in love and business. People came from all over the known world at the time to purchase these magic parchments, using them as amulets. Ephesus was also a sanctuary city for criminals and a center for sports, namely the Pan-Ionian games which is somewhat similar to our modern day Olympics. As a matter of fact today's Olympics is based on the Panhellenic Games of Ancient Greece.

Paul's victory in Ephesus was won in prayer in the spirit over the beasts of Ephesus

----

As you can see, Ephesus was no different to a modern city in the USA or Europe where godlessness, sports, witchcraft and heathenism reign. It is interesting to note that in our modern day, witchcraft, new age, psychic or fortune telling and false religions are revered but Christianity is disparaged. This is the work of the god of this world, who has blinded the eyes of the so-called educated people. There is a shroud or veil over them so that they cannot see. You would not think that educated people could be so stupid as to worship an idol or believe in witchcraft but many insanely do. Paul faced the same beast that we are facing today with more intense persecution – but he prevailed:

And this was known to all the Jews and Greeks also dwelling at Ephesus; and fear fell on them all, and the name of the Lord Jesus was magnified. And many that believed came, and confessed, and shewed their deeds. Many of them also which used curious arts brought their books together, and burned them before all men: and they counted the price of them, and found it fifty thousand pieces of silver. So mightily grew the word of God and prevailed.

ACTS 19:17-20

The structure and dynamics of Ephesus changed as Paul won the battles of the heavens. Souls were added to the kingdom and witchcraft took a beating as the power of God prevailed. Jesus, Daniel, Paul and Isaiah all revealed to us the power of prayer to rend the heavens to shake cities and nations. Now before we go to the next facet of prayer, let me inject another thought on rending the heavens. It is possible for the heaven to be closed and yet one person has an open heaven. While everybody is tasting the effects of a closed heaven, one person is enjoying a personal open heaven. In the same way the heaven can be open over an area and yet one person there is living under a closed heaven.

And thy heaven that is over thy head shall be brass, and the earth that is under thee shall be iron.

DEUTERONOMY 28:23

This Scripture further informs us that the heaven over a particular person's head or a particular nation can become brass, and the earth beneath, iron. This simply means that each individual and each country has an allocated air space above its head that can either be open or become brass. This is why you see certain people prosper in a difficult place while everybody else is struggling. One nation can be having revival while the neighboring nation is locked. You will also see this reality play out in the Scriptures:

> Jesus

Then cometh Jesus from Galilee to Jordan unto John, to be baptized of him. But John forbad him, saying, I have need to be baptized of thee, and comest thou to me? And Jesus answering said unto him, Suffer it to be so now: for thus it becometh us to fulfil all righteousness. Then he suffered him. And Jesus, when he was baptized, went up straightway out of the water: and, lo, the heavens were opened unto him, and he saw the Spirit of God descending like a dove, and lighting upon him

MATTHEW 3:13-16

As you see, it says the heavens were opened unto Jesus. It did not say it was open to everybody – only to Jesus – and the Holy Spirit lighted upon Him. There was a bunch of people who were baptized that day but only upon Jesus did the heaven open. In John 1:51, Jesus said to Nathaniel, '*...verily, verily, I say unto you, hereafter ye shall see heaven open, and the angels of God ascending and descending upon the Son of man.*' Jesus was also referencing Jacob in his statement.

> Jacob

After Jacob left his parent's abode while fleeing from his brother Esau, an interesting event took place:

*And he lighted upon a certain place, and tarried there all night, because the sun was set; and he took of the stones of that place, and put them for his pillows, and lay down in that place to sleep. **And he dreamed, and behold a ladder set up on the earth, and the top of it reached to heaven:***

and behold the angels of God ascending and descending on it. And, behold, the Lord stood above it, and said, I am the Lord God of Abraham thy father, and the God of Isaac: the land whereon thou liest, to thee will I give it, and to thy seed; And thy seed shall be as the dust of the earth, and thou shalt spread abroad to the west, and to the east, and to the north, and to the south: and in thee and in thy seed shall all the families of the earth be blessed. And, behold, I am with thee, and will keep thee in all places whither thou goest, and will bring thee again into this land; for I will not leave thee, until I have done that which I have spoken to thee of.

GENESIS 28:11-15

Jacob was tired and went to sleep. He used stones for a pillow. That stone is a type of Christ – He is our chief cornerstone (Ephesians 2:20) and the Rock (1 Corinthians 10:4). While he slept the heaven over him was opened and he saw angels going up and down. An open heaven releases angelic activities in your life and opens you up to the voice of God. We see that in the life of Jesus and Jacob here. An open heaven to Jacob resulted in God promising him the land and prosperity. It is no wonder that everything he touched turned into gold. Even when he was ill-treated by Laban, he prospered and even Laban prospered because of his association with Jacob. When the heaven over you is opened you will access the voice of God, prosper in whatever you put your hands to and there will be angelic activities in your life; you may not see the angels but you will see the manifestations of blessings in your life.

Each individual and each country has an allocated air space/ heaven above its head that can either be open or can become brass

❧ Ezekiel

The great prophet Ezekiel was among the captives in Babylon. That was not a pleasant experience for a Jew to go through. To the Israelites, the fact that they were in Babylon meant the judgment of God was a living reality. In a foreign land under the authority of foreign people, dispersed from their loved ones, it's no wonder they refused to sing the song of Zion in captivity:

> *By the rivers of Babylon, there we sat down, yea, we wept, when we remembered Zion. We hanged our harps upon the willows in the midst thereof. For there they that carried us away captive required of us a song; and they that wasted us required of us mirth, saying, Sing us one of the songs of Zion. How shall we sing the Lord's song in a strange land?*
>
> PSALM 137:1-4

As far as Israel was concerned, it was time to hang their harps upon the willow trees. No music, no fun, it was all gloom and doom... and yet something amazing happened:

> *Now it came to pass in the thirtieth year, in the fourth month, in the fifth day of the month, as **I was among the captives by the river of Chebar, that the heavens were opened, and I saw visions of God**. In the fifth day of the month, which was the fifth year of king Jehoiachin's captivity, **The word of the Lord came expressly** unto Ezekiel the priest...*
>
> EZEKIEL 1:19-3

Although Ezekiel was among the captives in Babylon, the heavens opened unto him and he saw visions of God and heard the voice of God expressly. While everyone else was feeling depressed, Ezekiel was experiencing an open heaven.

> The ladder and the angels

Both Jacob and Jesus mentioned the ladder and the ascending and descending angels. What is the significance? Please note how it is recorded in the Book of Beginnings and from the words of Jesus:

And he dreamed, and behold a ladder set up on the earth, and the top of it reached to heaven: and behold the angels of God ascending and descending on it.

GENESIS 28:12

And he saith unto him, Verily, verily, I say unto you, Hereafter ye shall see heaven open, and the angels of God ascending and descending upon the Son of man.

JOHN 1:51

The angels were ascending and descending. It did not say descending and ascending. Why is this important? The ascending and descending shows that the initiative starts from earth – that is through our prayers. Your prayers, just like the prayer of Jesus and Daniel will open up the heavens for you because God is no respecter of persons. A brass heaven results in an iron earth where nothing grows and everything becomes hard. This is why it is imperative for you to live and operate under an open heaven. Even the Lord Jesus did not do anything, did not minister, did not preach, did no miracles until the heaven was opened:

Now when all the people were baptized, it came to pass, that Jesus also being baptized, and praying, the heaven was opened, And the Holy Ghost descended in a bodily shape like a dove upon him, and a voice came from heaven, which said, Thou art my beloved Son; in thee I am well please.

LUKE 3:21-22

I want you to grasp that good things happen when the heavens are opened and bad things happen when the heavens are closed. Revival over a church is a result of an open heaven over that church.

The same is true over a city or nation. Moses unveiled to us the dire consequences of a closed heaven:

And I will break the pride of your power; and I will make your heaven as iron, and your earth as brass: And your strength shall be spent in vain: for your land shall not yield her increase, neither shall the trees of the land yield their fruits.

LEVITICUS 26:19-20

- ❖ Your strength will be spent in vain.
- ❖ Your land will not yield its increase – no harvest.
- ❖ Your trees in the land will not yield fruits – barrenness or fruitlessness.

Under a closed heaven your life will go in a circle; you will forever be moving but not getting anywhere. A closed heaven will result in a stagnant life. Your efforts and energies are wasted. A closed heaven will cause you to spend money without seeing the fruit of your purchase. Nothing will work for you yet they are working for others. Now let us look at some of the benefits of an open heaven:

- ❖ Access to the voice of God.
- ❖ The manifestation of the Holy Spirit.
- ❖ Breakthroughs.
- ❖ Bountiful harvest.
- ❖ Fruitfulness.

What is the key to an open heaven? Jesus had it! As Dr Luke informed us, *'Jesus also being baptized, and praying, the heaven was opened, And the Holy Ghost descended in a bodily shape...'*

Under a closed heaven, life is stagnant and going backwards. Your efforts and energies are wasted. There will be no satisfaction from what you invest. Everything goes sour. May that never be your portion.

Here are some keys that will open up the heaven for you:

❖ **Prayer will open the heaven** – This is why we pray, Jesus told us to pray for the will of God in heaven to be done upon the earth.

❖ **Fasting** – As Daniel prayed and fasted, the heaven was opened for the Angel to bring his answer to him after Michael was summoned to deal with the Prince of Persia.

❖ **Sacrificial giving** – '*Bring ye all the tithes into the storehouse, that there may be meat in mine house, and prove me now herewith, saith the Lord of hosts, if I will not open you the windows of heaven, and pour you out a blessing...*' (Malachi 3:10). Tithes and offerings open the heavens to dominate upon the earth.

❖ **Obedience to God** – Jesus said to John, '*Suffer it to be so now: for thus it becometh us to fulfil all righteousness*' (MATTHEW 3:15).

> *You need to pray for an open heaven over your life and destiny*

Good things happen when the heavens are opened
and bad things happen when the heavens are closed

CHAPTER 9
JESUS TEACHES DEPTHS AND DIMENSIONS IN PRAYER

Let my prayer be set forth before thee as incense; and the lifting up of my hands as the evening sacrifice.

PSALM 141:2

READING through the Gospels we know Jesus had depths and dimensions to his prayer life. We also know He was given to long stretches of time in prayer. There are depths and dimensions in prayer that most believers have never delved into. Because of a lack of knowledge, we let the enemy take advantage of us. Never forget, *the strength of your enemy is your ignorance and your silence.* Paul told the Corinthians that when we are ignorant of Satan's devices he gains an unfair advantage over us (2 Corinthians 2:11). Never forget, Adam's silence in the garden was the abdicating of his authority and position. So it is vitally important for you to know what the Word says and then pray the Word. Remember the angels said to Daniel: *'Fear not, Daniel: for from the first day that thou didst set thine heart to understand, and to chasten thyself before thy God, thy words were heard, and I am come for thy words'* (Daniel 10:12). His words were his prayers. We know that Daniel was a man given to much fasting and much prayers. We have it on record that he prayed three times daily:

Now when Daniel knew that the writing was signed, he went into his house; and his windows being open in his chamber toward Jerusalem, he kneeled upon his knees three times a day, and prayed, and gave thanks before his God, as he did aforetime.

DANIEL 6:10

Most Western believers struggle to pray once a day and this man was praying three times daily. The reason why we do not pray like Daniel and Jesus is because we have not been taught to pray. I did not say, 'have not been taught *how* to pray' because many of us know how to pray. Our problem is that we simply do not pray. Many have been taught the Word but not taught to pray. It is through teaching on prayer and praying that you catch the spirit of prayer. The more you pray the more efficient you will be at praying. In this chapter we will look at the teaching of Jesus on prayer. We will look at the depths and dimensions that he taught from the Gospel of Luke:

And it came to pass, that, as he was praying in a certain place, when he ceased, one of his disciples said unto him, Lord, teach us to pray, as John also taught his disciples. And he said unto them, When ye pray, say, **Our Father** *which art in heaven, Hallowed be thy name. Thy kingdom come. Thy will be done, as in heaven, so in earth. Give us day by day our daily bread. And forgive us our sins; for we also forgive every one that is indebted to us. And lead us not into temptation; but deliver us from evil. And he said unto them,* **Which of you shall have a friend, and shall go unto him at midnight, and say unto him, Friend,** *lend me three loaves; For a friend of mine in his journey is come to me, and I have nothing to set before him? And he from within shall answer and say, Trouble me not: the door is now shut, and my children are with me in bed; I cannot rise and give thee. I say unto you, Though he will not rise and give him, because he is his friend, yet because of his importunity he will rise and give him as many as he needeth. And I say unto you, Ask, and it shall be given you; seek, and ye shall find; knock, and it shall be opened unto you. For every one that asketh receiveth; and he that seeketh findeth; and to him that knocketh it shall be opened. If a son shall ask bread of any of you that is a father, will he give him a stone? or if he ask a fish, will he for a fish give him a serpent? Or if he shall ask an egg, will he offer him a scorpion? If ye then, being evil, know how to give good gifts unto your children: how much more shall your heavenly Father give the Holy Spirit to them that ask him?*

Luke 11:1-13

This exposé on prayer in the Gospel of Luke unveils different dimensions of prayer. First Jesus said to us when we pray say, 'Our father in heaven.' The first dimension of prayer that Jesus wanted us to tap into was relating to God as our father and this type of prayer is called *paternal prayer*.

What is paternal prayer?

Paternal prayer is when you address God as your Heavenly Father to meet your needs. He is your Abba Father and He wants to meet your needs. This is a basic dimension of prayer which every believer knows and is acquainted with. Jesus specifically said, *'If a son shall ask bread of any of you that is a father, will he give him a stone? or if he ask a fish, will he for a fish give him a serpent? Or if he shall ask an egg, will he offer him a scorpion?'* This has to do with our needs: God will meet our daily needs as our father. Jesus went on to say, *'If ye then, being evil, know how to give good gifts unto your children: how much more shall your heavenly Father give...'* . Let that sink into your spirit: *'how much more shall your heavenly Father give...'* He is a **much more** heavenly father! He is daddy God! Bread, fish and egg represent our daily needs. So on the paternal level of prayer, I am addressing God as my Father to meet my needs. There is nothing wrong with that. God wants to be your father and meet your needs as would a good earthly father, except that God will do much more. Paul reinforces this thought when he writes:

> *He that spared not his own Son, but delivered him up for us all, how shall he not with him also freely give us all things?*
>
> ROMANS 8:32

You have a right to have your needs met because God, the possessor of heaven and earth is your daddy. Paternal prayer is pretty much petitional prayer. Unfortunately that's all the level of praying that most believers are acquainted with but there are deeper dimensions. Let Jesus take you to the next dimension in prayer:

*And he said unto them, **Which of you shall have a friend, and shall go unto him at midnight, and say unto him, Friend,** lend me three loaves; For a friend of mine in his journey is come to me, and I have nothing to set before him?*

LUKE 11:5, 6

Jesus was still teaching on the subject of prayer but now He takes it to another dimension. He takes prayer from a paternal dimension to a *friend dimension*. The second dimension of prayer Jesus is getting us to understand is when we approach God on a friend level. To be more specific: on a covenant friend level. I am going to call this *fraternal prayer* and engage a French word, *amical* meaning 'friendly' and 'related to friends'.

What is fraternal prayer?

Fraternal prayer is when you address God on a covenant friend or brother level. Abraham was known as the friend of God (Isaiah 41:8, James 2;23). Jesus continues with his prayer exposé and opens up a scenario for us:

Imagine that one of your friends comes over at midnight. He bangs on the door and shouts, "Friend, will you lend me three loaves of bread? A friend of mine just showed up unexpectedly from a journey, and I don't have anything to feed him." Would you shout out from your bed, "I'm already in bed, and so are the kids. I already locked the door. I can't be bothered"? You know this as well as I do: even if you didn't care that this fellow was your friend, if he keeps knocking long enough, you'll get up and give him whatever he needs simply because of his brash persistence!

LUKE 11:5-8 THE VOICE

A man has a friend who comes to see him at midnight, which I am sure you will agree is a very inconvenient time. Now the man of the house has nothing to set before his friend. Have you ever been there? How many of us have no solution for people when they come to us with a problem? The man was in the same position that you likely find yourself in today –

he had nothing to assist his friend in his journey. So what did the man do? Thank God he had another friend that he could call upon. Let's make this picture even clearer for you.

Midnight Friend hungry – Host friend empty handed – Provision friend in bed.

Intercession

The host friend went to his provision friend on behalf of his visiting needy friend. Yes it was an inconvenient time but that did not stop the host friend from knocking on the door of his friend with the provision. This is a picture of intercession: the host friend is in the middle between his hungry visitor and the provision friend. He is standing in the gap. Although he had nothing in his house or his hands, he knew someone who had something and he went to that someone with fearless confidence on behalf of his hungry friend. When someone comes to you and you have nothing to set before them, don't get discouraged; you can go to your covenant friend and His name is God. He is more than willing to answer your call. In fact God is looking for intercessors:

> *The people of the land have used oppression, and exercised robbery, and have vexed the poor and needy: yea, they have oppressed the stranger wrongfully. And I sought for a man among them, that should make up the hedge, and stand in the gap before me for the land, that I should not destroy it: but I found none.*
>
> EZEKIEL 22:29-30

Jesus said that the man kept on knocking and would not relent until his friend on the inside came to meet his needs. The authorized version engages the word *importunity* while other translations use the words *brash persistence*. This is what intercession is: it is fearless and shameless confidence that will not be denied. This kind of attitude engages asking, seeking and knocking to get the desired manifestation. In other words if I don't get it by asking, I turn to seeking and if I don't see the desired results through asking and seeking, it means there must be a wall of opposition and so I take to knocking it down. Importunity means that you are shameless in your persistence and will not take no for an answer:

> *I have set watchmen upon thy walls, O Jerusalem, which shall never hold their peace day nor night: ye that make mention of the Lord, keep not silence, And give him no rest, till he establish, and till he make Jerusalem a praise in the earth.*
>
> ISAIAH 62:6-7

Do you have that kind of resolution when it comes to your family or friend who comes to you with a need? Fraternal prayer is when I engage God on the level of a covenant friend and I am willing to stand in the gap for another friend. I will stay before God and give Him no rest until He establishes what I am asking for. Now let's look at the third dimension in prayer that Jesus taught in the Gospel of Luke, which it is *judicial prayer*.

What is judicial prayer?

Judicial prayer is when you address God as your judge to give you justice because you feel a sense of wrongdoing committed against you:

> *And he spake a parable unto them to this end, that men ought always to pray, and not to faint; Saying, There was in a city **a judge, which feared not God**, neither regarded man: And there was a widow in that city; and she came unto him, saying, Avenge me of mine adversary. And he would not for a while: but afterward he said within himself, Though I fear not God, nor regard man; Yet because this widow troubleth me, I will avenge her, lest by her continual coming she weary me. And the Lord said, Hear what the unjust judge saith. And shall not God avenge his own elect, which cry day and night unto him, though he bear long with them? I tell you that he will avenge them speedily. Nevertheless when the Son of man cometh, shall he find faith on the earth?*
>
> LUKE 18:1-8

Judicial prayer is done when you feel a sense of injustice has been committed against you and you are being denied your rights.

Jesus was still teaching about prayer in the Gospel of Luke and He took us from the dimension of paternal prayer through fraternal prayer and now He takes us to another depth of prayer. At first He engaged the word 'father', then He took us to another word in prayer which was 'friend' and now He engages the word 'judge' in relation to prayer. Jesus was making a big contrast between an unjust judge and a righteous judge in God. The point to note was that they are both judges operating a court of law with legal cases. Jesus was teaching us that prayer is a court case that will be settled by a judge. This is why I call this kind of prayer *judicial prayer*. Judicial prayer is done when:

❖ You feel a sense of injustice has been committed against you.
❖ You are being denied your rights.
❖ You feel delayed.

The whole idea behind this parable is to pray non-stop and never surrender until the result manifests. The widow went to the unjust judge and said, '*Avenge me of mine adversary.*' The Amplified Bible said, '*Protect and defend and give me justice against my adversary.*' What do we know about this woman?

❖ **She was a widow** – meaning her husband was dead. His death may not have been natural as she called for justice.
❖ **She went to court** – evidently something illegal transpired which brought her to court.
❖ **She felt an act of injustice was committed against her** – now she was also asking for protection and claiming her rights.
❖ **She had an adversary** – bent on doing harm and injustice to her.
❖ **She was dealing with an unjust judge.**

I want you to notice the word *adversary* which in Greek is *antidikos*, a combination of two words, 'anti' meaning to 'deny' and 'against' and the word *dikos* meaning 'rights'. So when the two words are combined we understand that an adversary is one who will endeavor to deny us our rights. Who is our adversary? Peter rips off the veil to expose who it is in his epistle:

> *Be sober, be vigilant; because your adversary the devil, as a roaring lion, walketh about, seeking whom he may devour:*
>
> 1 PETER 5:8

The devil is the adversary and the one who will try to deny you your rights. The only way he can devour you is by denying you your rights. If you claim your rights, he cannot devour you. This is why you need judicial prayer.

The unjust judge delayed in giving justice to the widow but her persistence broke his imperviousness. In contrast, God is the righteous judge who is apt to give us justice from those who will deny us our rights. Abraham revealed the character of God to us when he said:

> *That be far from thee to do after this manner, to slay the righteous with the wicked: and that the righteous should be as the wicked, that be far from thee: **Shall not the Judge of all the earth do right?***
>
> GENESIS 18:25

The devil is the adversary and the one who will try to deny you your rights

------

The devil is called the accuser of the brethren and he accuses us with our past, our sins and transgressions, to deny us our rights. In effect he is the prosecuting attorney while Jesus is the defense attorney, ensuring that you receive your rights on the basis of the blood and the Word. See what John the Revelator said:

*And I heard a loud voice saying in heaven, Now is come salvation, and strength, and the kingdom of our God, and the power of his Christ: **for the accuser of our brethren is cast down, which accused them before our God day and night. And they overcame him by the blood of the Lamb, and by the word of their testimony;** and they loved not their lives unto the death.*

Revelation 12:10-11

We overcome Satan by the blood of the Lamb and the Word of our testimony. Jesus explained that if this widow resolved in her heart to never surrender to her adversary (the unjust judge) forcing him to give her justice, then how much more will God (the righteous judge) avenge us and make sure we have justice? These are the words of Jesus:

*And shall not God avenge his own elect, which cry day and night unto him, though he bear long with them? I tell you that **he will avenge them speedily**. Nevertheless when the Son of man cometh, shall he find faith on the earth?*

Luke 18:7

Preachers have preached the verses above with a view that God will have us in a holding pattern because He wants us to cry day and night. This is far from the truth! This verse is saying that to those who have resolved to cry before God day and night, He will avenge them speedily. Notice these words, '*he will avenge them speedily.*' God is not your problem, He will avenge you speedily but He needs to find faith to do so. Many are crying day and night with no faith, simply venting their unbelief to God and the devil.

> *We overcome Satan by the blood of the Lamb and the Word of our testimony*

Let us come boldly unto the throne of grace to obtain mercy and grace to help in time of need. Your Righteous Judge of the earth is sitting on that throne and He wants to stretch the scepter of favor over you but you have to pray judicial prayer in faith. Now let us go to the forth dimension of prayer which is *natal prayer*.

What is natal prayer?

Natal prayer is prayer to give birth to your destiny and the will of God in your life. We have come through paternal prayer, fraternal prayer, judicial prayer and now we must go to one of the deepest prayers in the Bible which is overlooked by so many believers and even ministers and that is natal prayer.

Natal prayer is travailing prayer, parturition prayer or laboring prayer to bring to birth the dream which was conceived and gestated. One very important point to understand is that there is a difference between the *plan* of God and the *will* of God. The plan of God, as it pertains to the ages will always come to pass but the will of God for a person may not necessarily manifest: it needs the co-operation of the individual. Many are not walking in the will of God because they have not given birth to it; they are carrying dreams and words in their spirits like a pregnant woman who gestated the baby but never gave birth. This is a most miserable situation to be in. To be heavily pregnant but never giving birth is very dangerous. Jesus, Paul, Epaphras, Isaiah and Elijah taught us on the subject of natal birth:

> *And he was withdrawn from them about a stone's cast, and kneeled down, and prayed, Saying, Father, if thou be willing, remove this cup from me: **nevertheless not my will, but thine, be done.** And there appeared an angel unto him from heaven, strengthening him. And being in an agony he prayed more earnestly: and his sweat was as it were great drops of blood falling down to the ground.*
>
> LUKE 22:41-44

> *He shall **see of the travail of his soul, and shall be satisfied:** by his knowledge shall my righteous servant justify many; for he shall bear their iniquities. Therefore will I divide him a portion with the great, and*

*he shall divide the spoil with the strong; because he hath poured out his soul unto death: and he was numbered with the transgressors; and he bare the sin of many, **and made intercession for the transgressors.***

ISAIAH 53:11-12

Jesus agonized in prayer in Gethsemane because He was travailing in intercession to see souls justified. The words *travail, labour* and *pangs* are words associated with pregnancy and we will see them in reference to prayer.

The plan of God as it pertains to the ages will always come to pass but the will of God for a person may not necessarily manifest because it needs the co-operation of the individual

In the Garden of Gethsemane, Jesus was agonizing and travailing in prayer for the will of God to be accomplished. Please notice the words '*being in an agony he prayed more earnestly*'. It took agonizing prayer to bring to pass the will of God. Similar to the agony a woman is in when she is giving birth, so is giving birth to the will of God. This is just the process of delivery of birth. I am not talking about suffering in sickness or pains of infirmities but the labor pains a woman goes through to bring the delivery of her child:

*Like as a woman with child, that draweth near the time of her delivery, is in pain, and crieth out in her pangs; so have we been in thy sight, O Lord. We have been with child, we have been in pain, we have as it were brought forth wind; we have not wrought any deliverance in the earth; neither have the inhabitants of the world fallen. Thy dead men shall live, together with my dead body shall they arise. Awake and sing, ye that dwell in dust: for thy dew is as the dew of herbs, and the earth shall cast out the dead. **Come, my people, enter thou into thy chambers, and shut*** *thy doors about thee: hide thyself as it were for a little moment, until the indignation be overpast.*

ISAIAH 26:17

> Epaphras and Paul

You will also notice that Epaphras and Paul were men given to natal prayers giving birth to the will of God and for Christ to be formed in believers:

*As ye also learned of **Epaphras our dear fellowservant, who is for you a faithful minister of Christ;** Who also declared unto us your love in the Spirit. For this cause we also, **since the day we heard it, do not cease to pray for you, and to desire that ye might be filled with the knowledge of his will** in all wisdom and spiritual understanding; That ye might walk worthy of the Lord unto all pleasing, being fruitful in every good work, and increasing in the knowledge of God; Strengthened with all might, according to his glorious power, unto all patience and longsuffering with joyfulness.*

COLOSSIANS 1:7-11

*Epaphras, who is one of you, a servant of Christ, saluteth you, **always labouring fervently for you in prayers, that ye may stand perfect and complete in all the will of God.***

COLOSSIANS 4:12

My little children, of whom I travail in birth again until Christ be formed in you

GALATIANS 4:19

Many are not walking in the will of God because they have not given birth to it

Natal prayers are needed to establish the will of God in a person, family or church. Paul also explained that when you see your church members being swayed with the whims and wiles of the world, it is time to travail in natal prayers until Christ is formed in them. You don't have to let carnality take over your church. You won't have a sin-benighted church if you travail in natal prayers for your members. Destinies are brought to birth when we pray natal prayers. See these words in Isaiah:

> *...This day is a day of trouble, and of rebuke, and of blasphemy: for the children are come to the birth, and there is not strength to bring forth.*
>
> ISAIAH 37:3

> *Before she travailed, she brought forth; **before her pain came, she was delivered** of a man child. **Who hath heard such a thing? who hath seen such things?** Shall the earth be made to bring forth in one day? or shall a nation be born at once? for as soon as Zion travailed, she brought forth her children. Shall I bring to the birth, and not cause to bring forth? saith the Lord: shall I cause to bring forth, and shut the womb? saith thy God.*
>
> ISAIAH 66:7-9

You cannot bring forth a child before travailing. There is no delivery of a child before some discomfort and pain. That's why we are asked a question, 'Who hath heard such a thing? who hath seen such things?' No one, but as soon as Zion travailed she brought forth her children! Zion represents the church and as soon as the church travails there will be souls added to the kingdom.

> ### Elijah

Perhaps the greatest example of natal prayer can be gleaned from the life of the praying power house prophet, Elijah. This man wielded power over the atmosphere and over the earth. He had great prowess in prayer. James, in his epistle, revealed how Elijah's prayer shut and opened the heaven:

> *The effectual fervent prayer of a righteous man availeth much. Elias was a man subject to like passions as we are, and he prayed earnestly that it might not rain: and it rained not on the earth by the space of three*

years and six months. And he prayed again, and the heaven gave rain,
and the earth brought forth her fruit.

JAMES 5:16-18

It's important to note, Elijah was not great in prayer *because* he was a simple man just like all of us. He had flaws and shortcomings like all of us but his strength was in praying to an Almighty God. Let's see how he opened the heaven for rain to come down after three and half years:

*And it came to pass after many days, that the word of the Lord came to Elijah in the third year, saying, Go, shew thyself unto Ahab; and I will send rain upon the earth. And Elijah went to shew himself unto Ahab. And there was a sore famine in Samaria...And Elijah said unto Ahab, Get thee up, eat and drink; for there is a sound of abundance of rain. So Ahab went up to eat and to drink. **And Elijah went up to the top of Carmel; and he cast himself down upon the earth, and put his face between his knees,** And said to his servant, Go up now, look toward the sea. And he went up, and looked, and said, There is nothing. And he said, Go again seven times. And it came to pass at the seventh time, that he said, Behold, there ariseth a little cloud out of the sea, like a man's hand. And he said, Go up, say unto Ahab, Prepare thy chariot, and get thee down, that the rain stop thee not. And it came to pass in the mean while, that the heaven was black with clouds and wind, and there was a great rain...*

1 KINGS 18:1-2, 41-45

In the third year of no rain, the word of the Lord came to Elijah, '*Go show yourself before King Ahab and I will send rain.*' Now you would think that when he showed up before King Ahab that there would be rain. Is that what happened? Not really! Look what it said:

And Elijah went to shew himself unto Ahab. And there was a sore famine in Samaria...

1 KINGS 18:2

I thought that God said, 'Show yourself before the king and I will send rain.' Elijah did and there was no rain! Did God lie or did Elijah miss it? No, absolutely no! The Word of the Lord came to Elijah but he would have to give birth to that word. When you receive a word from God you have received a seed in your spirit and this word, like a seed must be given birth to. Here's how Elijah did it: '*And Elijah went up to the top of Carmel; and he cast himself down upon the earth, and put his face between his knees...*' Why did the Bible deem it important for you to know the physical posture of Elijah when he prayed?

To you and to me it means nothing that he cast himself down and put his face between his knees. In those days that was the position women put themselves in to give birth. So in effect, Elijah put himself in the birth position, engaged in natal prayer to bring to birth the delivery of the word that God gave him. At the seventh time his servant reported the size of the cloud to him, he said, '*Behold, there ariseth a little cloud out of the sea, like a man's hand.*' When Elijah got into the birthing position in prayer, God Himself was ready to catch the delivery of the child. This is why the servant saw the cloud as the hand of a man. When you engage in natal prayer, God Himself will be the midwife to bring about the safe delivery of your destiny. Remember the word *midwife* is not gender-related but profession-related, meaning someone who has studied midwifery. Elijah was going through labor pains seven times as he pushed that word out. You will experience that when you are a seasoned praying person. Sometimes it is like having contraction pains and you are praying and groaning in the spirit as a woman in labor. Seasoned prayer warriors know this phenomenon as they pray in tongues to bring to birth the destiny of churches and nations.

No man or woman who taps into natal prayer will have their destinies be still-born or aborted

I want to encourage you to tap into the dimension of natal prayer and bring forth your destiny. You will feel like you are in agony in your praying when you do so and it simply means that you are going through labor pains and pangs. No man or woman who taps into natal prayer will have their destinies be still-born or aborted. It is time for the delivery of your destiny. Jesus did it, Elijah, Paul and Epaphras did it and so can you!

You cannot bring forth a child before travailing

You need to realize that when Jesus revealed these dimensions and depths in prayers that he was also revealing maturing in our prayer lives. The reason many do not delve into these realms of prayers is because they have a very shallow prayer life centered on themselves and their needs. However as you tap into intercessory prayers you are tapping into the heart of God because you are tapping into the present day ministry of Jesus. You see praying for someone else, praying for your city, church, nation and praying to give birth to the will of God in the earth is taking your eyes off of you. Remember, God is looking for intercessors. He is looking for people who will have this kind of resolution in prayer:

> *I have set **watchmen** upon thy walls, O Jerusalem, **which shall never hold their peace day nor night: ye that make mention of the Lord, keep not silence, And give him no rest, till he establish**, and till he make Jerusalem a praise in the earth.*
>
> ISAIAH 62:6-7

Watchmen are intercessors: they watch over friend, family, church, city, nation and the will of God to be established. God says we are to cry day and night and give Him no rest until the will of God for Jerusalem or your city, church and family is established and there is a praise and an aroma of life from our city, church and family.

Watchmen are intercessors

There is a need for you to mature in your prayer life and let this be said about you:

Issachar is a strong ass couching down between two burdens: And he saw that rest was good, and the land that it was pleasant; and bowed his shoulder to bear, and became a servant unto tribute.

GENESIS 49:14-15

A donkey speaks of one who carries weights and burdens. Today believers do not want to hear about carrying a burden for the Lord. We think this means a lack of faith. The old timers knew this meant they would have to *pray through*. Once you couch between the burdens of prayer then you will see the land will be pleasant and the rest, good. It is time to develop and mature in prayer in order to bring to birth the words and plans that God has for your life.

CHAPTER 10
ALONE WITH GOD

As you peruse the pages of the synoptic Gospels you will find that Jesus often withdrew and spent alone-time to pray and be with the Father. Although He was very busy in ministry He deliberately made time to be alone. He loved to be in a deserted and solitary place with his Father:

When Jesus heard of it, he departed thence by ship into a desert place apart: and when the people had heard thereof, they followed him on foot out of the cities.

MATTHEW 14:13

And in the morning, rising up a great while before day, he went out, and departed into a solitary place, and there prayed.

MARK 1:35

But Jesus often withdrew to lonely places and prayed.

LUKE 5:18 NIV

And it came to pass in those days, that he went out into a mountain to pray, and continued all night in prayer to God.

LUKE 6:12

The life of Jesus teaches us to take pleasure in time alone with God. His life teaches us that privacy and solitude with God deepens the relationship and enables effectiveness in public ministry. This simply means *the efficacy of your private devotions will determine public delights*. While there is tremendous benefits in corporate gatherings before God, nothing takes the place of alone-time with God. Our relationship with God is therefore not only a communal affair but a personal affair. All relationships take time and the first principle of relationship is *whatever you are willing to invest in is what you will harvest.* In other words, how much you put in is how much you will get out. A relationship with God is no different in that it still follows the same fundamental principles of relationships. A marriage will be in decline if the husband and wife are never alone together, so will the vitality of our fellowship with God if we keep neglecting our time with Him. Any man who will spend time alone with God will return in the power of the Spirit of God. Aloneness and power go together. I did not say loneliness but aloneness. We see this in the lives of Jesus, Jacob, Moses, Paul, Peter and Daniel to name a few. Jesus taught us that the key to effective prayer is praying in the secret place of intimacy with the father:

> *But thou, when thou prayest, enter into thy closet, and when thou hast shut thy door, pray to thy Father which is in secret; and thy Father which seeth in secret shall reward thee openly.*
>
> MATTHEW 6:6

The life of Jesus teaches us to take pleasure in time alone with God

The uncommon grace that is shed when one is in solitude with God is intoxicating. David revealed the uncommon grace that is shed upon a man who seeks God in the desert and solitary place. Here's an overview of Psalm 63 from the Prince of Preachers, Charles Haddon Spurgeon:

> **A Psalm of David, when he was in the wilderness of Judah. This was probably written while David was fleeing from Absalom; certainly at the time he wrote it he was king (Psalms 63:11), and hard pressed by those who sought his life. David did not leave off singing because he was in the wilderness, neither did he in slovenly idleness go on repeating Psalms intended for other occasions; but he carefully made his worship suitable to his circumstances, and presented to his God**

a wilderness hymn when he was in the wilderness. *There was no desert in his heart, though there was a desert around him.* We too may expect to be cast into rough places ere we go hence. In such seasons, may the Eternal Comforter abide with us, and cause us to bless the Lord at all times, *making even the solitary place to become a temple for Jehovah.* The distinguishing word of this Psalm is EARLY. When the bed is the softest we are most tempted to rise at lazy hours; but when comfort is gone, and the couch is hard, if we rise the earlier to seek the Lord, we have much for which to thank the wilderness.

TREASURY OF DAVID

O God, thou art my God; early will I seek thee: my soul thirsteth for thee, my flesh longeth for thee in a dry and thirsty land, where no water is; **To see thy power and thy glory,** *so as I have seen thee in the sanctuary. Because thy lovingkindness is better than life, my lips shall praise thee. Thus will I bless thee while I live: I will lift up my hands in thy name.* **My soul shall be satisfied as with marrow and fatness; and my mouth shall praise thee with joyful lips:** *When I remember thee upon my bed, and meditate on thee in the night watches. Because thou hast been my help, therefore in the shadow of thy wings will I rejoice. My soul followeth hard after thee: thy right hand upholdeth me. But those that seek my soul, to destroy it, shall go into the lower parts of the earth. They shall fall by the sword: they shall be a portion for foxes. But the king shall rejoice in God; every one that sweareth by him shall glory: but the mouth of them that speak lies shall be stopped.*

PSALM 63:1-11

Jacob was also a man who knew the power of being alone with God. He discovered that being alone in prayer gives a man prevailing power with God and man. I am sure you remember that after Jacob deceived his father Isaac and stole the blessing from Esau, the latter was none to pleased and decided that he would kill Jacob:

And Esau hated Jacob because of the blessing wherewith his father blessed him: and Esau said in his heart, The days of mourning for my father are at hand; then will I slay my brother Jacob. And these words of Esau her elder son were told to Rebekah: and she sent and called Jacob her younger son, and said unto him, Behold, thy brother Esau, as touching thee, doth comfort himself, purposing to kill thee.

GENESIS 27:41, 42

> *The uncommon grace that is shed when one is in solitude with God is intoxicating*

The same spirit of murder that was in Cain – who killed Abel – was now lodged in Esau and he was biding for the right time to kill Isaac. This evil intention spurred Rebekah to send Jacob away. He went away for over twenty years. Then after twenty years expired he decided to go back home but he was petrified because he knew there was a death assignment over his life:

*And Jacob sent messengers before him to Esau his brother unto the land of Seir, the country of Edom. And he commanded them, saying, Thus shall ye speak unto my lord Esau; Thy servant Jacob saith thus, I have sojourned with Laban, and stayed there until now: And I have oxen, and asses, flocks, and menservants, and womenservants: and I have sent to tell my lord, that I may find grace in thy sight. And the messengers returned to Jacob, saying, **We came to thy brother Esau, and also he cometh to meet thee, and four hundred men with him. Then Jacob was greatly afraid and distressed:** and he divided the people that was with him, and the flocks, and herds, and the camels, into two bands;*

GENESIS 32:3-7

As you can see from the above verses, Jacob was distressed and in fear because his brother had gathered a 400-man army to come and meet him. So he divided his family into two groups so that if Esau attacked one group, the other could escape. Then we read something very interesting:

And Jacob was left alone; and there wrestled a man with him until the breaking of the day. And when he saw that he prevailed not against him, he touched the hollow of his thigh; and the hollow of Jacob's thigh was out of joint, as he wrestled with him. And he said, Let me go, for the day breaketh. And he said, I will not let thee go, except thou bless me.

GENESIS 32:24-26

Jacob was alone with God in prayer and he wrestled all night long in prayer. What was the end result?

And he said unto him, What is thy name? And he said, Jacob. And he said, Thy name shall be called no more Jacob, but Israel: for as a prince hast thou power with God and with men, and hast prevailed. And Jacob asked him, and said, Tell me, I pray thee, thy name. And he said, Wherefore is it that thou dost ask after my name? And he blessed him there. And he said, Thy name shall be called no more Jacob, but Israel: for as a prince hast thou power with God and with men, and hast prevailed.

GENESIS 32:27-29

And Jacob lifted up his eyes, and looked, and, behold, Esau came, and with him four hundred men. And he divided the children unto Leah, and unto Rachel, and unto the two handmaids. And he put the handmaids and their children foremost, and Leah and her children after, and Rachel and Joseph hindermost. And he passed over before them, and bowed himself to the ground seven times, until he came near to his brother. And Esau ran to meet him, and embraced him, and fell on his neck, and kissed him: and they wept.

GENESIS 33:1-4

This is what you need to grasp: there was a death assignment over the life of Jacob. The hatred Esau had for Jacob had brewed for twenty years and did not subside. When he knew Jacob was on his way back, he went with four hundred men to finish what he had in his heart. However Jacob spent the whole night alone with God in wrestling prayers. Jacob had a divine encounter that caused him to say he had seen the face of God. He was then blessed and a prophetic word was released over him: '*Thy name shall be called no more Jacob, but Israel: for as a prince hast thou power with God and with men, and hast prevailed.*' Then next thing that we see after his divine encounter is Esau meeting Jacob. There is quite a contrast in their encounter: '*And Esau ran to meet him, and embraced him, and fell on his neck, and kissed him: and they wept.*' Instead of killing his brother, Esau is now hugging and embracing his little brother. What happened? While Jacob was alone with God, he wrestled in prayer and disarmed the spirit of murder on Esau.

The fundamental principle of relationship is whatever you are willing to invest is what you will harvest

---

Alone with God in prayer gives you prevailing power with God and man.

Alone with God in prayer gives you prevailing power over the heavens and the earth.

Alone with God in prayer gives you power to disarm your enemies.

Alone with God in prayer gives you power to subpoena/summon the enemy before Heavenly Justice.

We see many others in the Bible who spent time alone with God. Moses was alone with God on the mountain when he encountered the burning bush (Exodus 3). Zacharias was alone with God when he learned he would be the father of John the Baptist (Luke 1:5-20). Paul spent much alone time with God and was loaded with revelation knowledge. He was the one who taught us the authority of the believer, righteousness by faith, the gifts of the Spirit, the virtues of praying in tongues and the fruit of the Spirit to name a few. So your alone time with God is not wasted time but a time of refreshing, refinement and impartation. The world talks about solitary confinement of a misbehaving prisoner in jail as a form of punishment. To be alone with God is not confinement but refinement. In that place of solitude will be the place of plenitude. To exhibit supernatural power in public it is prerequisite for a man to be alone in God's presence. There is just no two ways around it.

Your alone time with God is not wasted time but a time of refreshing, refinement and impartation

Let's once again look to our Lord. We are gleaning from His prayer life to develop ours. Yes He took Peter, James and John with Him to pray but these three guys were busy sleeping. You will discover that the disciples had a hard time catching up with the prayer life of Jesus. He would wake up really early to pray and He would spend long periods of time in prayer, in desert places or in the mountain. He prioritized His alone time with God above ministry to people because He knew that to be effective before people He would need the presence and power of God. This is because He was operating in the earth as a man anointed with the Holy Spirit. All the miracles which He did were done as a man led by the Spirit and walking by faith. Even though He was God manifested in the flesh – He was fully God and fully man – in the earth He operated as a man. This is why He was so dependent upon God. Here's an example for you:

But so much the more went there a fame abroad of him: and great multitudes came together to hear, and to be healed by him of their infirmities. And he withdrew himself into the wilderness, and prayed.
                                                              LUKE 5:15-16

Now if that was most modern preachers, they would think they have hit the jackpot or got it made when the great multitude came to hear them yet Jesus withdrew into the wilderness to pray. You can imagine the shock and dismay of the disciples when they saw what He did. Jesus placed ministering unto God and ministry from God above ministry to people. We have it backwards: we place ministry to people above ministering to God and you cannot have effective ministry to people without first being alone with God. With all the demands upon Him, Jesus deliberately withdrew Himself. He made a conscious decision to do so. What was the end result?

> *And it came to pass on a certain day, as he was teaching, that there were Pharisees and doctors of the law sitting by, which were come out of every town of Galilee, and Judæa, and Jerusalem:* **and the power of the Lord was present to heal them.**
>
> LUKE 5:17

Withdrawing from public to be in private with the Father will result in power being present to heal and deliver. When Jacob was alone with God, he was led into the path of high places and goodness:

> *So the Lord alone did lead him, and there was no strange god with him. He made him ride on the high places of the earth, that he might eat the increase of the fields; and he made him to suck honey out of the rock, and oil out of the flinty rock;*
>
> DEUTERONOMY 32:12-13

Alone with God is solitary refinement

§ Our bone of contention

The issue for most believers is that we do not like being alone in prayer because we do not know how to handle being on our own and talking to someone we cannot see, hear and feel. When you are in a conversation with another human being you can physically see, feel and hear them so it's easy to spend time in their presence because of the interaction. How do you spend time with someone you cannot see and interact with?

I love what the great revivalist Jonathan Edwards wrote many years ago. He captured the modern believer's disposition:

> Some are greatly affected when in company; but have nothing that bears any manner of proportion to it in secret, in close meditation, prayer and conversing with God when alone, and separated from the world. A true Christian doubtless delights in religious fellowship and Christian conversation, and finds much to affect his heart in it; but he also delights at times to retire from all mankind, to converse with God in solitude. And this also has peculiar advantages for fixing his heart, and engaging his affections. True religion disposes persons to be much alone in solitary places for holy meditation and prayer... It is the nature of true grace, however it loves Christian society in its place, in a peculiar manner to delight in retirement, and secret converse with God.
>
> THE WORKS OF JONATHAN EDWARDS,
> VOLUME 2: RELIGIOUS AFFECTIONS

The footnotes to this paragraph in this volume are even more engaging, revealing and enlightening:

> The Lord is neglected secretly, yet honored openly because there is no wind in their chambers to blow the sails; and therefore they stand still. Hence many keep their profession, when they lose their affection. They have by the one a name to live, (and that is enough), though their hearts be dead...They were warm only by another's fire, and hence having no principle of life within, soon grow dead.
>
> THOMAS SHEPARD, AMERICAN PURITAN MINISTER

We can see the minister's and the believer's present conundrum: do we do what Thomas Shepard stated, in that we honor the Lord publicly but neglect him privately? Are we warmed up by another's fire or do we have the fire of God burning within us?

I know you may feel frustrated at the fact that you don't know how to be alone with God. So, how do you spend time with someone you cannot see and interact with? Sometimes you may feel, 'Am I even being heard here?' Or 'Am I just talking to myself here?' As you mature you can begin to hear His voice and interact with Him but prior to that it seems like agony to just sit there and pray to the unseen. The thing you must realize is that *you are being heard even when you feel that this is a waste of time.* Let me remind you of Thomas who, after the Resurrection when Jesus appeared to the disciples the first time in the assembly room was not present with them:

> **But Thomas, one of the twelve, called Didymus, was not with them when Jesus came.** *The other disciples therefore said unto him, We have seen the Lord.* **But he said unto them,** *Except I shall see in his hands the print of the nails, and put my finger into the print of the nails, and thrust my hand into his side, I will not believe.*
>
> JOHN 20:24-25

Thomas was adamant that the Lord did not appear to the disciples. He probably thought they were pulling a fast one on him. Besides that, the last time he saw Jesus, He was crucified and had died. So he made this bold declaration, '*Except I shall see in his hands the print of the nails, and put my finger into the print of the nails, and thrust my hand into his side, I will not believe.*' Now let's see what happened eight days later:

> *And after eight days again his disciples were within, and* **Thomas with them:** *then came Jesus, the doors being shut, and stood in the midst, and said, Peace be unto you.* **Then saith he to Thomas, Reach hither thy finger, and behold my hands; and reach hither thy hand, and thrust it into my side:** *and be not faithless, but believing. And Thomas answered and said unto him, My Lord and my God.*
>
> JOHN 20:26-28

When Jesus came into the room the first time, Thomas was not there physically; when Thomas came into the room saying what he said,

Jesus was not there physically. Isn't it interesting that when Jesus appeared the second time, He quoted the words of Thomas verbatim? This means even though He was not there physically *He heard the words of Thomas because He is omnipresent.* Likewise you must have this in your thinking that the Lord hears every word that you utter in prayer. In essence what Jesus was conveying to His disciples after the Resurrection was the need to be conscious of His abiding presence, irrespective of their feelings. The time between the Resurrection and the Ascension was forty days, as revealed by Dr Luke:

> *To whom also he shewed himself alive after his passion by many infallible proofs, being seen of them forty days, and speaking of the things pertaining to the kingdom of God:*
>
> ACTS 1:3

For forty days the disciples did not know when Jesus would appear to them or when He would come and go. This was not like before when they would wake up and He was there with them. For three and a half years they tracked His every movement. Now Jesus was training them to not focus on His physical presence – which they were so used to – but on His inward, abiding presence. The constant, unannounced comings and goings for forty days were getting them ready for the time when He would eventually go and not return. Then on the day of Ascension we read:

> *And when he had spoken these things, while they beheld, he was taken up; and a cloud received him out of their sight. And while they looked stedfastly toward heaven as he went up, behold, two men stood by them in white apparel; Which also said, Ye men of Galilee, why stand ye gazing up into heaven? this same Jesus, which is taken up from you into heaven, shall so come in like manner as ye have seen him go into heaven.*
>
> ACTS 1:9-11

He had weaned them from their craving for His constant physical presence to His spiritual invisible presence and He told them, *'lo, I am with you alway, even unto the end of the world'* (Matthew 28:20).

How do I spend time alone with God?

Now that we have talked a little bit about the importance of being alone with God, the question remains, 'How do I spend quality alone time with God?' We live in a modern world where there are too many things vying for our attention. We are bombarded on a daily basis with noise, entertainment, traffic, phone calls, texts, emails, Instagram, WhatsApp, Internet, friends, children, spouse clamoring for our attention. All of social media and the prevalence of smart phones are designed to keep our lines of communication open. The lines are open to everyone but God; we do not give God the time of day; He is an after-thought. One thing you must know about God is that He will never wrestle with you for your time. If you want to deepen your relationship with Him then you have to make time for quality fellowship with Him. Here are some steps for you to develop alone time with God:

❖ Make the deliberate decision to block time for you and God. Time blocking is an effective time management tip to gain time and allow you to be in charge of what you want done. Decide how long you will be in His presence. It may be you want to spend one hour daily, so you have to block out the time and stick to it. Make it a daily routine.

❖ If you are just too busy in the day and cannot seem to make the time then be like Jesus and have an early session with God. Early risers escape the hustle and bustle of a hectic day. It is not easy because your flesh will not like it. So if you decide to rise early, you will need to get out of bed because the temptation to fall back to sleep will be too much for you to handle.

❖ Find a place in your house where you will regularly meet with God. It is your special place with God. Some people like to go for a walk and that will work too.

❖ Do not take your cell phone and iPad with you because you will be tempted to check your emails, texts and other messages. You want to be free from distractions. Avoid distraction at all cost. I have a room in my house which I call the Holy Room and there is nothing in there to distract me. The room only has two sofas and a little table.

❖ It is imperative to have your Bible. God will speak to you through His Word. You can also take a music player that will play worship music and a notepad to write down impressions, thoughts and words that come into your spirit. That's about the only three things you should take with you.

❖ Don't be frustrated when you first start if you find yourself bored. Your flesh will hate it but you are training it to be silent before God. Most of the time it will be the noise inside of you that will break your focus on God. All the ideas, plans and thoughts that will run through your mind when you decide to be in God's presence are simply a ploy of the enemy to sidetrack you. Solitude prayer is like going to the gym and going through your circuit. It looks monotonous and boring but something is happening to set you up for a better future. So don't let your mind tell you that it is futile.

❖ Spend time worshiping, praying, confessing and reading your Bible. The predominant way that God will speak to you is through His Word. Read His Word and you will notice some verses will start jumping out at you. That is what is called a quickened word.

❖ What I do when I am in my Holy Room is just take my Bible and pen. I like to play some soft instrumental hymns or soft worship music because I want an atmosphere of worship. I am very picky about the kind of music I listen to when I am spending time alone with God. Some songs, as great as they are simply irritate me. I find that soft instrumental worship and soft worship music create an atmosphere conducive for me to spend time in His presence.

❖ You can take a prayer list and pray it before the Lord. When you become serious and continue in your alone time with God you will discover that after your time of worship and adoration you will then begin to bring your petitions before God. As time goes by the Spirit of intercession will get a hold of you and you will pray some things through. You will bring your most pressing needs and you will quickly see that the time in His presence has increased.

In a nutshell, your alone time with God should be in a secret place and a secret hour with no distraction, characterized by adoration, meditation and petition, which will lead to direction, instruction and unction.

Time alone with Him will be characterized by adoration, meditation and petition which will lead to direction, instruction and unction

CHAPTER 11
JESUS TEACHES THE PRAYER OF IMPORTUNITY

IT is of great importance to understand that attached to the prayer of importunity is the key to great breakthroughs. The people who have seen major breakthroughs have been those who faithfully prayed, with persistent and importunate prayers. It takes the prayer of importunity to resist, regain and repossess lost ground when all the demons of hell are in opposition. It is crucial for you to realize that it was Jesus himself who taught importunity in prayer:

> *And he said unto them, Which of you shall have a friend, and shall go unto him at midnight, and say unto him, Friend, lend me three loaves; For a friend of mine in his journey is come to me, and I have nothing to set before him? And he from within shall answer and say, Trouble me not: the door is now shut, and my children are with me in bed; I cannot rise and give thee. I say unto you, Though he will not rise and give him, because he is his friend, yet **because of his importunity** he will rise and give him as many as he needeth. And I say unto you, Ask, and it shall be given you; seek, and ye shall find; knock, and it shall be opened unto you. For every one that asketh receiveth; and he that seeketh findeth; and to him that knocketh it shall be opened.*
>
> LUKE 11:5-10

Let's remind ourselves that Jesus is giving this illustration after one of His disciples asked Him, '*Lord teach us to pray.*' We already discovered that this dimension of prayer is fraternal prayer – where you meet God on a level of covenant friend, to meet the need of another friend. Now I want to focus on a word that Jesus engaged in this illustration and that is the word *importunity*:

I say unto you, Though he will not rise and give him, because he is his friend, yet because of his importunity he will rise and give him as many as he needeth.

LUKE 11:8

We have to add another of Jesus' illustrations to the story above in order to fully grasp the prayer of importunity:

And he spake a parable unto them to this end, that men ought always to pray, and not to faint; Saying, There was in a city a judge, which feared not God, neither regarded man: And there was a widow in that city; and she came unto him, saying, Avenge me of mine adversary. And he would not for a while: but afterward he said within himself, Though I fear not God, nor regard man; Yet because this widow troubleth me, I will avenge her, lest by her continual coming she weary me. And the Lord said, Hear what the unjust judge saith. And shall not God avenge his own elect, which cry day and night unto him, though he bear long with them? I tell you that he will avenge them speedily. Nevertheless when the Son of man cometh, shall he find faith on the earth?

LUKE 18:1-8

See these words, '*And he spake a parable unto them to this end, that men ought always to pray, and not to faint...*' The purpose of this parable was to illustrate that we must always be persistent and never give up in prayer. Jesus taught this parable with the intention of provoking men and women from faintheartedness, weakness and a lackadaisical attitude in prayer to persistent prayer. Persisting in prayer is not a lack of faith but a *whack* of faith against opposition, doubt and the devil. These two accounts show us the feats of the prayer of importunity.

What exactly is the prayer of importunity? We do not hear much about this type of prayer these days, nonetheless it is a reality because Jesus talked about it. While there are volumes of books about the *prayer of faith* there are just few books on the *prayer of importunity* except from the old timers.

Isn't it interesting that when Jesus was ask to expound on His prayer life He broached the prayer of importunity after relational or paternal prayer?

§ Defining Importunity

Different translations employ different terms to explain importunity and they are:

* ❖ Shameless audacity.
* ❖ Persistence.
* ❖ Keeps on making request.
* ❖ Sheer persistence.
* ❖ Shameless confidence.
* ❖ Fearless confidence.
* ❖ Audacity.
* ❖ Aggressive asking.
* ❖ Undeniable assertiveness.
* ❖ Shameless boldness.
* ❖ Relentless demand.

> *It is interesting to note when Jesus was ask to expound on His prayer life He broached the prayer of importunity after relational prayer*

The prayer of importunity is the kind of prayer that will not bow or surrender until the answer manifests. I want to release a statement in your spirit. Meditate upon these words and let them permeate your thinking. *'Importunate – persistent – shameless confident prayer is needed to defy the antagonism and hostile obstruction to your destiny.'* I am going to insert a quote from my book, 'Provoking Exploits through the Force of Imposing Aggressive Faith' on the power of the prayer of importunity. I want to give you eight awesome secrets of importunate prayer and add some additional thoughts to them:

1 **Importunate prayer is the art of dealing and appealing to the friendship of God on behalf of another friend** – We see this in the parable: the man goes to his friend at midnight on behalf of his other friend. The little Syrophenician woman approached Jesus on behalf of her daughter. The father whose son was a lunatic approached Jesus on his behalf. Jairus approached Jesus on the behalf of his stricken daughter.

2 **Importunate prayer is a shameless and inconvenient urgency that persists in request and petition until it is granted** – It is not moved by negativity or opposition, it just keeps on praying no matter what. The Syrophenician woman shamelessly persisted even though Jesus told her, '*...for it is not meet to take the children's bread, and to cast it unto the dogs*' (Mark 7:27). Her reply was absolute gold and provoked Jesus to move, '*Yes, Lord: yet the dogs under the table eat of the children's crumbs*' (Mark 7:28). She did not care that she was a Gentile, out of covenant and out of dispensation. She did not care that she was called a dog. Irrespective of being called a dog and being out of covenant and dispensation, she got her miracle simply because of importunity. It takes long distance faith to develop this brand of prayer. This is not short distance faith as expressed through Peter when he was walking on the water and wilted when he saw the effects of the wind and waves. The prayer of importunity keeps walking no matter the waves or wind simply because Jesus said to '*come*'.

3 **Importunate prayer engages 'asking, seeking and knocking' until the answer manifests** – Asking is petitioning, seeking is supplicating and knocking is interceding. It moves through these dimensions of prayer to obtain its objectives. The prayer of importunity is not bothered if it asked and did not see immediate results because it realizes there are oppositions. So if asking does not get the job done, then it goes through the seeking avenue and if that does not work it will engage knocking and keep on knocking until the wall of opposition is down.

4 **Importunate prayer is prayer that grows in intensity, perseverance and tenacity** – You remember when it said of Jesus, '*And being in an agony he prayed more earnestly: and his sweat was as it were great drops of blood falling down to the ground*' (Luke 22:44). Jesus pressed in prayer. Importunate prayer presses into God when the going gets rough. It will not back down when the pressure intensifies. When the devil realizes that you will not back down then he will have to back down. The unjust judge had to change his attitude towards the widow woman simply because she would not change her posture.

5 **Importunate prayer is not bothered by the 'passed time' or 'too late' factor** – The 'too late' factor is not even a factor; it just goes and gets the job done. The man did not care that it was already passed bedtime. He did not care that he would inconvenience his friend at midnight. Lazarus was dead and in the grave for four days and his body was already stinking. Did that sway Jesus in any shape? Not at all he kept on praying. The widow woman did not care that she was dealing with an unjust judge. She kept pressing until justice was granted. There is nothing to late for the prayer of importunity.

6 **Importunate prayer is prayer that is relentless until it receives** – The prayer of importunity will never take no for an answer. It is the intercession of the Spirit of God, in us and through us that will make tremendous power available. It is wrestling in prayer until the will and plans of God are established in the earth. This wrestling in prayer is not determined by the decibels of the voice but with the intent and heartfelt desires of the heart.

7 **Importunate prayer is the effectual, fervent prayer of the righteous that makes tremendous power available, to ensure that justice is rendered** – James, the brother of Jesus told us, '*The effectual fervent prayer of a righteous man availeth much*' (James 5:16). James could say that because he saw it in the prayer life of Jesus. He saw how, between major miracles Jesus spent long stretches of time in prayer.

8 **Importunate prayer is prayer that possesses the gates of your enemies, dethroning principalities** – The words *importunate, importunity, opportune* and *opportunity* have the same etymology: *Portus*, meaning 'harbor'. Opportunity is from the Latin word *opportunus*, from *ob* - 'in the direction of' and *portus* - 'harbor', originally describing the wind driving toward the harbor, hence 'seasonable.' Importunity is from the Latin word *importunus* meaning 'inconvenient, unseasonable,' based on Portunus, the name of the god who controlled and protected harbors (from portus 'harbor') – Oxford English Dictionary.

So when we tap into the prayer of importunity we are removing the *god of gates* that commands what comes in and goes out. Many times in our lives, things that should be coming in are not coming in and what should be leaving are not leaving. It can happen on a personal, familial and national level so it looks like we are constantly out of season. Importunate prayer makes that which is out of season to be in season. Jericho was a prime example of a stronghold of no one coming in and going out. Look at the words of Moses:

And we took all his cities at that time, there was not a city which we took not from them, threescore cities, all the region of Argob, the kingdom of Og in Bashan. All these cities were fenced with high walls, gates, and bars; beside unwalled towns a great many. And we utterly destroyed them, as we did unto Sihon king of Heshbon, utterly destroying the men, women, and children, of every city. But all the cattle, and the spoil of the cities, we took for a prey to ourselves.

DEUTERONOMY 3:4-7

The walls, bars and gates were destroyed and they took the spoil of the cities. Through importunate prayer you will destroy the walls, bars and gates and take the spoil. God is no respecter of persons; He will back you up. Great exploits come from importunate prayer. Praying the prayer of importunity helps us to fulfill a promise God made to Abraham, '*...thy seed shall possess the gate of his enemies*' (Genesis 22:17). It is when you possess the gates that you have influence.

§ Importunity and Opportunity

You will notice what we have in common between the words im*portunity* and op*portunity* is *portunity*. I want to submit to you that the more you pray the prayer of *importunity*, the more new *opportunities* it will create for you. Opportunities that you would never have had will be heading towards you as you tap into this marvelous dimension of prayer. It takes shameless, boldface faith to persist in prayer. Keep praying and you will defy the odds and win.

Importunate prayer is a mighty movement of the soul toward God. It is a stirring of the deepest forces of the soul, toward the throne of heavenly grace. It is the ability to hold on, press on, and wait – E.M Bounds

Before we close this chapter, I have to deal with a mental block that is in the head of many Spirit-filled or Word-filled people's minds. For years we were told that if we pray about a situation more than one time then we are in unbelief. So with that in mind, people are scared to pray about a situation more than one time. The idea of the prayer of importunity, or praying through has become a foreign idea to modern believers and this has sapped away at a prayer life which, for the most part has become non-existent.

To be honest with you, the modern church as we see it in the West today is at its weakest when it comes to praying. We have a lot of eloquence and plenty of charismatic personalities but few people that can bring heaven down.

❯ Is it unbelief to pray more than one time?

One of the things we have to address is the idea that you only need to pray about a situation one time and if you do more than one time then you are in unbelief. We run into problems when we appropriate one principle of prayer to all other principles of prayer. There are different rules of engagement in prayer and you cannot make a sweeping statement that in all situations you only pray one time. This just shows ignorance of the subject matter on a bigger scale.

Just as we mentioned before that there are different golf clubs to deal with different shots, so there are different engagement techniques in our prayer bag. Let us answer the question then. In the Garden of Gethsemane we see Jesus presented the same petition three times:

> *Then cometh Jesus with them unto a place called Gethsemane, and saith unto the disciples, Sit ye here, while I go and pray yonder. And he took with him Peter and the two sons of Zebedee, and began to be sorrowful and very heavy. Then saith he unto them, My soul is exceeding sorrowful, even unto death: tarry ye here, and watch with me.* **And he went a little farther, and fell on his face, and prayed, saying, O my Father, if it be possible, let this cup pass from me: nevertheless not as I will, but as thou wilt.** *And he cometh unto the disciples, and findeth them asleep, and saith unto Peter, What, could ye not watch with me one hour? Watch and pray, that ye enter not into temptation: the spirit indeed is willing, but the flesh is weak.* **He went away again the second time, and prayed, saying, O my Father, if this cup may not pass away from me, except I drink it, thy will be done.** *And he came and found them asleep again: for their eyes were heavy.* **And he left them, and went away again, and prayed the third time, saying the same words.** *Then cometh he to his disciples, and saith unto them, Sleep on now, and take your rest: behold, the hour is at hand, and the Son of man is betrayed into the hands of sinners. Rise, let us be going...*
>
> MATTHEW 26:36-46

> *And they came to a place which was named Gethsemane: and he saith to his disciples,* **Sit ye here, while I shall pray.** *And he taketh with him Peter and James and John, and began to be sore amazed, and to be very heavy; And saith unto them, My soul is exceeding sorrowful unto death: tarry ye here, and watch. And he went forward a little, and fell on the ground, and prayed that, if it were possible, the hour might pass from him. And he said, Abba, Father, all things are possible unto thee; take away this cup from me: nevertheless not what I will, but what thou wilt.*

*And he cometh, and findeth them sleeping, and saith unto Peter, Simon,
sleepest thou? couldest not thou watch one hour? Watch ye and pray, lest
ye enter into temptation. The spirit truly is ready, but the flesh is weak.
And again he went away, and prayed, and spake the same words. And
when he returned, he found them asleep again, (for their eyes were heavy,)
neither wist they what to answer him. And he cometh the third time, and
saith unto them, Sleep on now, and take your rest: it is enough, the hour
is come; behold, the Son of man is betrayed into the hands of sinners.*

MARK 14:32-41

Jesus prayed about the same thing three times. If we apply the logic that
praying about something more than once is unbelief then we will need
to accuse Jesus of unbelief. I do not think anyone of us would ever say
such a thing about Jesus! We see here that Jesus was on a prayer watch
in Gethsemane. When the Lord said *watch and pray* He was not implying
anything to do with watching your wristwatch when you pray.

In Bible days a *watch* referred to a three-hour segment such as 6pm-9pm
or 9pm-12 am. The term *watch* also referred to watchmen who relieved each
other at the end of these periods. Jesus was in importunate prayer for three
hours and it was so intense that it brought him to a point of sweating blood.
The question still remains, '*Did it indicate unbelief when Jesus used the same
words?*' No! So why did Jesus keep praying and praying and saying the
same things? Jesus was travailing in prayer until He broke through. Those
prayers would sustain Him through the trials, beatings and assaults that
He would later receive. He had won the battle during importunate prayer in
Gethsemane. Let's look at another great man of prayer and his name is Elijah:

*...The effectual fervent prayer of a righteous man availeth much. Elias
was a man subject to like passions as we are, and **he prayed earnestly
that it might not rain:** and it rained not on the earth by the space of three*

*years and six months. **And he prayed again, and the heaven gave rain,** and the earth brought forth her fruit.*

JAMES 5:16-18

Elijah was a great man of prayer and he had great power with God and the atmosphere. Through his prayer the heaven closed and there was no more rain for three and a half years. Then the apostle James said, '*He prayed again and the heaven gave rain.*' So with that in mind, let us look at how he prayed:

*And Elijah said unto Ahab, Get thee up, eat and drink; for there is a sound of abundance of rain. So Ahab went up to eat and to drink. **And Elijah went up to the top of Carmel; and he cast himself down upon the earth, and put his face between his knees,** And said to his servant, Go up now, look toward the sea. And he went up, and looked, and said, There is nothing. And he said, Go again seven times. And it came to pass at the seventh time, that he said, Behold, there ariseth a little cloud out of the sea, like a man's hand. And he said, Go up, say unto Ahab, Prepare thy chariot, and get thee down, that the rain stop thee not. And it came to pass in the mean while, that the heaven was black with clouds and wind, and there was a great rain.*

1 KINGS 18:41-45

Notice these words, '*And Elijah went up to the top of Carmel; and he cast himself down upon the earth, and put his face between his knees...*' What was Elijah doing? He was in prayer mode. Like we already discovered, Elijah was in the birthing process through natal prayer. The point I want to bring across to you is, 'How many times did he pray?' The answer was in his request to his servant, '*Go up now, look toward the sea. And he went up, and looked, and said, There is nothing.*' How many times did Elijah tell him to go? Seven times. This simply means he prayed about the same situation seven times. Therefore if Elijah prayed seven times about the same situation, are you going to say that Elijah was in unbelief? No, Elijah was in importunate prayer too. There are things that need the importunate prayer of asking, seeking and knocking.

When I am dealing with personal needs, I just pray one time and thank God for it but when I am praying about destiny and there are things that need shifting, I will attack it over and over in prayer until the spiritual resistance is broken. I want to encourage you to pray until something happens!

Persistence breaks resistance

CHAPTER 12

CONTENDING FOR PROPHECIES THROUGH SPIRITUAL WARFARE

FINALLY as we come to the last chapter of this book, I want to look at a very important aspect of prayer, which is *spiritual warfare*. When we were looking at the different aspects of the prayer life of Jesus we saw that He engaged prayer as a weapon of spiritual warfare. Understand that this whole thing began with a war in heaven in the Pre-Adamite world and will end with a war at the wrapping up of the end-of-days. If you do not like war then you will not like the Bible because it is a book of war: spiritual wars which manifest in physical wars. The so-called modern church wants to sweep spiritual warfare under the carpet but the true church of Jesus Christ understands it is in conflict with unseen spiritual entities. Therefore you need to be aware of the reality of spiritual warfare and here is the crux of spiritual warfare, which came right out of the mouth of Goliath:

> *If he be able to fight with me, and to kill me, then will we be your servants: but if I prevail against him, and kill him, then shall ye be our servants, and serve us.*

> 1 SAMUEL 17:9

Goliath said, *'If I take him out then you serve us but if you take me out then we will bow and be your subjects'* This is the vivid reality of your present life, ministry and city. If you do not deal with these unseen powers then you will be subject to them. Look at countries which are in revival and where the church is thriving; it is because they dealt with the long-seated principality over that nation in prayer. The church, through spiritual warfare unseated the principality, which had the people as its subjects. Whether you like it or not that is just the way it goes. The reason why your children are suffering is because you never took the enemy out when you had the chance. There can be no conquest without conflict and confrontation. Conquest comes after confrontation. Do not be afraid of the devil; you already have all of the armor of God and all the weapons that you need to enforce victory.

There are two trains of thought when it comes to spiritual warfare and you can find them from the book of Numbers; the twelve spies that were sent to the Promised Land:

> We are not able and they will eat us up

But the men that went up with him said, We be not able to go up against the people; for they are stronger than we. And they brought up an evil report of the land which they had searched unto the children of Israel, saying, The land, through which we have gone to search it, is a land that eateth up the inhabitants thereof; and all the people that we saw in it are men of a great stature. And there we saw the giants, the sons of Anak, which come of the giants: and we were in our own sight as grasshoppers, and so we were in their sight.

NUMBERS 13:31-33

You will find this weak attitude in many believers today. The ten spies bought an evil report of the good land which God gave them; they had a *grasshopper complex*. With their mouths they said their enemies will eat them up. Many believers are afraid to tap into spiritual warfare because they feel that it would upset demons and principalities. The truth is these principalities *need* to be disturbed and dislodged from their strongholds otherwise, as Goliath said, we will be serving them. Read through your Bible and you will discover that for Israel to take the land they had to confront long-standing occupants already present. Although they looked ferocious and were very stubborn – as in the case of Og, the King of Bashan – when Israel went after them, God gave them victory. By the way the name *Og* means 'stubborn'. He was the King of Bashan and he had people and land:

And when ye came unto this place, Sihon the king of Heshbon, and Og the king of Bashan, came out against us unto battle, and we smote them: And we took their land, and gave it for an inheritance unto the Reubenites, and to the Gadites, and to the half tribe of Manasseh.

DEUTERONOMY 29:7-8

> Let us go up at once, they are bread for us. We can eat them up.

*And Caleb stilled the people before Moses, and said, **Let us go up at once**, and possess it; **for we are well able to overcome it...** Only rebel not ye against the Lord, **neither fear ye the people of the land; for they are bread for us: their defence is departed from them, and the Lord is with us: fear them not.***

NUMBERS 13:30; 14:9

Unlike the ten spies who saw themselves as prey, Joshua and Caleb saw themselves as the predators who can eat the occupiers of their Promised Land. That is the kind of attitude you need to possess. When you are aggressive in prayer you will find the same things that occurred in Deuteronomy will be yours:

*Then we turned, and went up the way to Bashan: and Og the king of Bashan came out against us, he and all his people, to battle at Edrei. And the Lord said unto me, Fear him not: for **I will deliver him, and all his people, and his land, into thy hand;** and thou shalt do unto him as thou didst unto Sihon king of the Amorites, which dwelt at Heshbon. So **the Lord our God delivered into our hands Og also, the king of Bashan, and all his people: and we smote him until none was left to him remaining. And we took all his cities at that time, there was not a city which we took not from them, threescore cities, all the region of Argob, the kingdom of Og in Bashan.** All these cities were fenced with high walls, gates, and bars; beside unwalled towns a great many. And we utterly destroyed them, as we did unto Sihon king of Heshbon, utterly destroying the men,* *women, and children, of every city. But all the cattle, and the spoil of the cities, we took for a prey to ourselves. And we took at that time out of the hand of the two kings of the Amorites the land that was on this side Jordan, from the river of Arnon unto mount Hermon;*

DEUTERONOMY 3:1-8

Notice these words, '*we took at that time out of the hand of the two kings of the Amorites the land that was on this side Jordan, from the river of Arnon unto mount Hermon;*' You need to take the land out of the hand of the enemy; you need to take your children out of the hand of the enemy. God is waiting on you. He will back you up. As Paul said to Timothy, '*Fight the good faith of faith and lay hold of eternal life*' (1 Timothy 6:12). This means that you cannot lay hold of eternal life, the more abundant life until you contend in warfare.

*Life does not give you what you deserve
but what you contend for*

Warfare is important: life does not give you what you deserve but *what you fight for*. Esau deserved the blessing of the double portion but did not get it. Reuben deserved the double portion but did not get it. The lesson is simple: *life does not give you what you deserve but what you contend for*. The great apostle Paul unveiled an aspect of warfare that will do you good to pay attention to:

Wherefore we would have come unto you, even I Paul, once and again; but Satan hindered us.

1 THESSALONIANS 2:18

For we wanted to come to you--certainly I, Paul, did, again and again – but Satan blocked our way.

N.I.V

For we wanted to come to you (I, Paul, in fact tried again and again) but Satan thwarted us.

NET BIBLE

You can't imagine how much we missed you! I, Paul, tried over and over to get back, but Satan stymied us each time.

THE MESSAGE

Because it was our will to come to you. [I mean that] I, Paul, again and again [wanted to come], but Satan hindered and impeded us.

AMPLIFIED BIBLE CLASSIC EDITION

The word *hindered* is rendered as 'opposed, thwarted, blocked, resisted, foiled' and 'withstood'. It is the Greek word *egkopto,* meaning 'to cut into', to impede one's course by cutting off his way. Now we realize this is the great apostle Paul who used this word. This is the same man who taught us about the authority of the believer, the man who shook the snake back in the fire and the man who said, *'And the God of peace shall bruise Satan under your feet shortly'* (Romans 16:20). This is the man who fought the beast of Ephesus and won, now revealing that Satan foiled, opposed and resisted his attempt to go to a place. This shows you that the adversary, or Satan will oppose you and try to stop you from entering into your destiny. Was this a sole event in the Scriptures or do we have examples of this phenomenon happening with other people?

> Daniel

Then said he unto me, Fear not, Daniel: for from the first day that thou didst set thine heart to understand, and to chasten thyself before thy God, thy words were heard, and I am come for thy words. But the prince of the kingdom of Persia **withstood me** *one and twenty days: but, lo, Michael, one of the chief princes, came to help me; and I remained there with the kings of Persia.*

DANIEL 10:12-13

Daniel was a man of the Book: in Daniel 9 we have record of him reading the book of Jeremiah. We know he was also a man of prayer because we have a record of him praying three times daily: *'Now when Daniel knew that the writing was signed, he went into his house; and his windows being open in his chamber toward Jerusalem, he kneeled upon his knees three times a day, and prayed, and gave thanks before his God, as he did aforetime'* (Daniel 6:10). We also know that he was a man given to much fasting, as we see through the book of Daniel. He was concerned with the destiny of Israel and the succeeding world powers till the end times. He was on a prayer and fasting season to get some answers and the angel said to him, *'When you prayed the answer was released but the Prince of Persia resisted me.'* Who was the Prince of Persia? It was not the king who ruled at the time but the principality behind his administration. Daniel's prayer was being resisted and obstructed by that demon. I want you to be aware of these words, 'hindered, opposed and withstood'. We have seen it in Paul's and Daniel's lives.

---

*The adversary or Satan will oppose you
entering into your destiny*

> Moses

Now as Jannes and Jambres withstood Moses, so do these also resist the truth: men of corrupt minds, reprobate concerning the faith. But they shall proceed no further: for their folly shall be manifest unto all men, as theirs also was.

2 TIMOTHY 3:8-9

Here is something that we did not read in the Pentateuch but that the apostle Paul unveiled it to us. Jannes and Jambres were not mentioned anywhere in the Old Testament and yet Paul revealed their opposition to the ministry of Moses. The question remains, 'Who were Jannes and Jambres that they withstood Moses?' They were the chief wizards and sorcerers of Pharaoh. Moses had an encounter with God where he was given a Rhema word:

'*Let my people go.*' You would think that when he walked into Egypt with that Rhema word with his rod of signs and wonders that Pharaoh would let the people go. On the contrary, Pharaoh resisted and then engaged Jannes and Jambres to resist and obstruct Moses. They used sorceries and witchcraft to oppose the ministry of Moses.

> Paul and Barnabas

So they, being sent forth by the Holy Ghost, departed unto Seleucia; and from thence they sailed to Cyprus. And when they were at Salamis, they preached the word of God in the synagogues of the Jews: and they had also John to their minister. And when they had gone through the isle unto Paphos, they found a certain sorcerer, a false prophet, a Jew, whose name was Bar-jesus: Which was with the deputy of the country, Sergius Paulus, a prudent man; who called for Barnabas and Saul, and desired to hear the word of God. But Elymas the sorcerer (for so is his name by interpretation) withstood them, seeking to turn away the deputy from the faith. Then Saul, (who also is called Paul,) filled with the Holy Ghost, set his eyes on him, And said, O full of all subtilty and all mischief, thou child of the devil, thou enemy of all righteousness, wilt thou not cease to pervert the right ways of the Lord? And now, behold, the hand of the Lord is upon thee, and thou shalt be blind, not seeing the sun for a season. And immediately there fell on him a mist and a darkness; and he went about seeking some to lead him by the hand.

ACTS 13:4-11

Remember, this is after a season of fasting and prayer and after being commissioned for the work of the ministry, with hands being laid upon them that Paul and Barnabas went to preach. What do we see? Their preaching or their Gospel was being opposed by Elymas the Sorcerer. Paul did not entertain and accommodate his resistance but dealt with him swiftly. This is why Paul told the saints in Thessalonica: '*Finally, brethren, pray for us, that the word of the Lord may have free course, and be glorified, even as it is with you*' (2 Thessalonians 3:1). Prayer is what gives the Word free course to bring forth fruit in ministry and in church. I am amazed to see many ministers not realizing that their Gospel will be opposed and resisted. Spiritual opposition is a reality. Here are four important points you need to consider:

* Paul was resisted and opposed on a personal level.
* Daniel was resisted and opposed on a national level.
* Moses was resisted and opposed on a ministerial level.
* Paul and Barnabas were resisted and opposed in the preaching of the Gospel.

You need to realize that the enemy will also oppose, hinder and resist you on these different levels too. If he opposed Paul, he certainly will oppose you. He will resist you on a:

* Personal level.
* Familial level.
* Professional level.
* Ministerial level.

Satan will do his best to thwart and subvert your destiny but here is God's thought toward this opposition:

To subvert a man in his cause, the Lord approveth not.
                                                LAMENTATIONS 3:36

The Lord does not approve when a man's destiny is subverted and boycotted. The Lord does not approve of the sabotage of your destiny. He does not approve of your business, career, life or family being subverted. So if the Lord does not approve, then you must not approve. In addition to that, see what Paul said:

Now as Jannes and Jambres withstood Moses, so do these also resist the truth: men of corrupt minds, reprobate concerning the faith. But they shall proceed no further...
                                                2 TIMOTHY 3:8-9

If the Lord does not approve, then you must not approve

'They shall proceed no further...' – this must be your resolve today. You must tell the devil and anything negative that is in motion in your life today: '*You will proceed no further.*' Every wizard or sorcerer resisting your ministry or church must surrender before you. Do not play with them, let this thought be in your mind: '*Thou shalt not suffer a witch to live*' (Exodus 22:18). This must be your resolve, '*Devil, if you are going to tangle with me, you will be fighting a losing battle.*'

Many years ago, I heard Jesse Duplantis sing this song, 'Me and the devil had a tussle but I won. Me and the devil, we don't agree. I hate the devil, he hates me. Me and the devil had a tussle but I won.' You see the devil loves the path of least resistance. Notice in the scripture the words *proceed further*. Where did we see these words before?

> Now about that time Herod the king stretched forth his hands to vex certain of the church. And he killed James the brother of John with the sword. And because he saw it pleased the Jews, he **proceeded further** to take Peter also.
>
> ACTS 12:1-3

Notice in Acts 12, the devil, through Herod proceeded further but Paul in Timothy said they shall proceed no further. Which one is a reality in your life? Is he proceeding further or is he proceeding no further? If you do not put a stop to the devil, he will proceed further. In Acts 12 the church finally stopped the proceeding further of the enemy when they resorted to prayer:

> Peter therefore was kept in prison: but prayer was made without ceasing of the church unto God for him.
>
> ACTS 12:5

'Me and the devil had a tussle but I won. Me and the devil, we don't agree, I hate the devil, he hates me. Me and the devil had a tussle but I won' – Jesse Duplantis

---

Unceasing and long stretches of prayer were made on behalf of Peter, causing his deliverance. In fact the Greek text would read as, '*extended and protracted prayer was made of the church unto God for him.*' The church warred in prayer to stop Satan from taking another pillar from the church after he took James. If the church did not pray unceasingly, Peter would have gone the way of James even though he had a prophetic word from Jesus that he would live to be an old man:

> *Verily, verily, I say unto thee, When thou wast young, thou girdedst thyself, and walkedst whither thou wouldest: **but when thou shalt be** old, thou shalt stretch forth thy hands, and another shall gird thee, and carry thee whither thou wouldest not.*
>
> JOHN 21:18

This is where so many people miss it. They think just because they have received a prophetic word that it will automatically come to pass. Many have received prophetic words and died without seeing the fulfillment because they were under the notion that prophecies are automatic. Look at what Paul said to Timothy:

> *This charge I commit unto thee, son Timothy, according to the prophecies which went before on thee, that thou by them mightest war a good warfare;*
>
> 1 TIMOTHY 1:18

§ What is a prophetic word?

Prophecies are weapons of warfare to fulfill destinies. A weapon is an instrument to be engaged in battle – in an offensive fashion – to slay the enemy, thus bringing about the desired result. Paul was endeavoring to get Timothy to understand that he had many prophecies over his life but it was up to him to use them as mighty weapons of warfare to tear down strongholds and opposition. A prophecy must be a wielded weapon in spiritual warfare to bring forth a God-given destiny. Attached to a prophetic word is a prophetic destiny. This is why you must take spiritual warfare seriously. Let me give you seven descriptions of what it is and why you must take spiritual warfare seriously.

1 SPIRITUAL WARFARE IS WARFARE WITH INVISIBLE BEINGS, SPIRITS WITHOUT BODIES THAT WILL SEEK TO HINDER YOUR DESTINY

You cannot see them but they are the emissaries of Satan with a mission to frustrate your destiny. This is why Paul said: *'For we wrestle not against flesh and blood, but against principalities, against powers, against the rulers of the darkness of this world, against spiritual wickedness in high places'* (Ephesians 6:12). You have a God-given destiny which you must fulfill on the earth and their mission is to thwart your attempt at that destiny. We tend to look at problems in non-spiritual terms, then try to resolve these issues from non-spiritual positions. Everything that transpires in the visible is a reflection of wars being waged in the unseen realm with invisible beings. The repercussions of the ongoing battles in the unseen world are manifested in the negativity that you are experiencing, with the chief culprit being unseen beings such as principalities, powers, rulers of the darkness of this world and wicked spirits in heavenly places. Their whole agenda is to block, thwart, obstruct, delay, destroy, oppose, resist and hinder you in your destiny.

Attached to a prophetic word is a prophetic destiny

2 SPIRITUAL WARFARE IS WARFARE WITH SPIRITS WHO ARE AGAINST YOUR PROGRESS AND SUCCESS

You have been called to be a partaker of divine nature and to a life of glory and virtue. Therefore success is to be the hallmark of your life. You, as every other human being are under the first command of Elohim to the Adamic race: *'Be fruitful and multiply...'* (Genesis 1:28).

God has called you to unlimited success but it will not be an easy ride. You will be fought against and there will be many adversaries as Paul revealed: *'For a great door and effectual is opened unto me, and there are many adversaries'* (1 Corinthians 16:9). Notice a great and effectual door was opened to Paul but there were adversaries in the way of his walking through that opened door. It is not that the door was closed but that there were many oppositions and hindrances to him walking through an open door. In the book of Revelation we are told: *'behold, I have set before thee an open door, and no man can shut it...'* (Revelation 3:8). God has opened many doors for you but there are stumbling blocks and hindrances that you need to remove in order to walk through them. These spirits are there to impede your progress and success.

3 SPIRITUAL WARFARE IS WARFARE WITH THE SPIRITS OF DELAY AND DETAINMENT OF YOUR PROPHETIC DESTINY

These emissaries of the evil one will seek to delay or detain you in a place of stagnancy. One of the tactics of the devil is to delay you if he cannot kill you. His objective is to kill you to get you out of his way but if he cannot do that then he will obstruct, oppose, detain and delay. He knows delaying you will be a source of great frustration. He knows exasperation will make you want to give up on your prophetic destiny. Every believer has a prophetic destiny.

> What is a prophetic destiny?

A prophetic destiny is you walking in the fulfillment of God's promises or in the fulfillment of a personal word of prophecy which may have come through an individual or a word that God dropped in your spirit. All the promises of God in the Scriptures are to bring you to your prophetic destiny. Every prophetic word that you have received is an unfolding of your prophetic future and destiny. However the fulfillment of your prophetic destiny is not automatic because if it were all believers would be walking in the fullness of God and you know as you look around that this is not a reality in millions of believer's lives. This is why Daniel had to pray through the promises made to Israel in the book of Jeremiah concerning the end of captivity:

> *For thus saith the Lord, That after seventy years be accomplished at Babylon I will visit you, and perform my good word toward you, in causing you to return to this place. For I know the thoughts that I think toward you, saith the Lord, thoughts of peace, and not of evil, to give you an expected end.*
>
> JEREMIAH 29:10-11

All the promises of God in the Scriptures are to bring you to your prophetic destiny. Every personal prophetic word that you have received is an unfolding of your prophetic future and destiny

You would think that when the seventy years was over, the children would automatically walk out. That is not what transpired. Daniel had to pray and fast: '*In the first year of his reign I Daniel understood by books the number of the years, whereof the word of the Lord came to Jeremiah the prophet, that he would accomplish seventy years in the desolations of Jerusalem. And I set my face unto the Lord God, to seek by prayer and supplications, with fasting, and sackcloth, and ashes...*' (Daniel 9:2-3). If there is delay and detainment of your destiny, it indicates that you have not engaged spiritual warfare.

In Genesis God told Abraham: '*Know of a surety that thy seed shall be a stranger in a land that is not theirs, and shall serve them; and they shall afflict them four hundred years*' (Genesis 15:13). Stephen echoed the same promise that God made to Abraham in his sermon in Acts:

> *And God spake on this wise, That his seed should sojourn in a strange land; and that they should bring them into bondage, and entreat them evil four hundred years.*
>
> ACTS 7:6

The reality on the ground was that Israel was delayed longer:

Now the sojourning of the children of Israel, who dwelt in Egypt, was four hundred and thirty years.

EXODUS 12:40

God said four hundred years but they were there for four hundred and thirty years. Did God lie? Never! God never makes mistakes. The mistake is always on the human side and never on the divine side. The error was on Moses' part who moved ahead of God by ten years and then had to deal with Pharaoh who was stubborn and delayed them. By the time Moses took them out of Egypt he was 80 years old and Israel was in its 430th year of captivity, which means when Moses was 40 years, Israel was in its 390th year of captivity. He tried to move ahead of God and messed the whole plan because he did so in the flesh by killing an Egyptian.

The Exodus also had its roots in spiritual warfare; it could not be a reality without praying and doing warfare:

And it came to pass in process of time, that the king of Egypt died: and the children of Israel sighed by reason of the bondage, and they cried, and their cry came up unto God by reason of the bondage. And God heard their groaning, and God remembered his covenant with Abraham, with Isaac, and with Jacob. And God looked upon the children of Israel, and God had respect unto them.

EXODUS 2:23-25

Groaning refers to intercession and praying as we see in Paul's epistle to the Romans and Jesus' experience with Lazarus (Romans 8:26, John 11:33,38). These examples remind me of what the great preacher, John Wesley said:

'It seems that God will not do anything until his people pray'

To see the fulfillment of your prophetic destiny, it is time to fight in prayer.

4 SPIRITUAL WARFARE IS FIGHTING A NEGATIVE INVISIBILITY TO CREATE A POSITIVE VISIBILITY

Let us once and for all deal with what some would say: 'Now brother, I am not a fighter but a lover. I am resting in Jesus.' To which I say 'Amen but our problem is not Jesus it is the devil'. Yes, we are resting in Jesus but we are in conflict with Satan and his cohorts. That is the reality. You as a believer – and we as the church, or body of Christ – are in direct conflict with wicked spirits. There cannot be conquest without conflict. Whatever you are not willing to confront, you will not conquer. The whole of the Old Testament was given us as ensamples:

Now all these things happened unto them for ensamples: and they are written for our admonition, upon whom the ends of the world are come.

1 CORINTHIANS 10:11

They had to fight to enter their Promised Land. Never once should you think that the Promised Land was a type of heaven. It was not because there were giants to overcome there. In heaven there are no giants to overcome. The Promised Land is a *type* of their prophetic destiny and they had to contend for it. This is why we say *spiritual warfare is fighting a negative invisibility to create a positive visibility*. Many are oblivious to the negative atmosphere over them and they are subject to evil forces and restrictions because they have never fought to change the atmosphere above them to create a positive environment below.

Whatever you are not willing to confront you will not conquer

5 SPIRITUAL WARFARE IS FIGHTING UNSEEN REAL POWERS TO CREATE A BETTER PRESENT AND A BETTER FUTURE

Paul explicitly told us, '*For though we walk in the flesh, we do not war after the flesh: For the weapons of our warfare are not carnal, but mighty through God to the pulling down of strong holds*' (2 Corinthians 10:3-4).

We live in the physical but it is the unseen realm that is pulling the strings. There are evil forces, demonic powers that are seeking to unseat you and make your future miserable. Let this be known to you that you not only have power but you also have authority, which puts you in a position of command. See what God said to Israel:

> *Rise ye up, take your journey, and pass over the river Arnon: behold, I have given into thine hand Sihon the Amorite, king of Heshbon, and his land: begin to possess it, and contend with him in battle.*
>
> DEUTERONOMY 2:24

God said, '*I have given into your hand but possess it by contending for it.*' To us this does not make sense: '*Why should I fight for something that God gives me?*' The instruction to Moses could be written as: '*You have to contend for the land because someone else is occupying it presently; there is someone on your land and you need to move him*'. It is the same for us. God has given us the land but we need to contend for it because the enemy is presently occupying it. This occupying agent is unseen and through spiritual warfare we take the land to create a better present. Your fight is with unseen forces who are bent on stopping you. Our warfare is done through prayer, confession and fasting.

On the other side of the coin, if you maintain the prayer pressure, the battles in the heavenlies are won and the ramification will manifest positively for you in the physical world. We see this in the steadfast petition of Daniel, which eventually broke the resistance of the Prince of Persia and enabled the angel to deliver the message to him (Daniel 10). Another great example of how things are shaped for our betterment in the spirit world can be seen in the death of the mighty commander Sisera:

> *And the children of Israel again did evil in the sight of the Lord, when Ehud was dead. And the Lord sold them into the hand of Jabin king of Canaan, that reigned in Hazor; the captain of whose host was Sisera,*

which dwelt in Harosheth of the Gentiles. And the children of Israel cried unto the Lord: for he had nine hundred chariots of iron; and twenty years he mightily oppressed the children of Israel.

JUDGES 4:1-3

It was a bleak time in the history of Israel who, for twenty years was oppressed by King Jabin's commander, Sisera. His ruthless rule was enforced by the fact that he had nine hundred iron war chariots. These chariots were considered the most advanced weapons of mass destruction at that time. These war chariots were drawn by ten horses with each chariot carrying a driver and four archers. The chariot also had a sheath on each side loaded with extra bows and hundreds of arrows. Iron scales armored the sides of the chariots and the heavy wheels had scythes that were 1 meter (3 feet) long, which would spin and cut the opposing soldiers into pieces. Sisera looked and felt unstoppable. How was he stopped? At the time there was a prophetess by the name of Deborah and she released a prophetic word:

*And Deborah, a prophetess, the wife of Lapidoth, she judged Israel at that time. And she dwelt under the palm tree of Deborah between Ramah and Beth–el in mount Ephraim: and the children of Israel came up to her for judgment. And she sent and called Barak the son of Abinoam out of Kedesh–naphtali, and said unto him, **Hath not the Lord God of Israel commanded, saying, Go and draw toward mount Tabor, and take with thee ten thousand men of the children of Naphtali and of the children of Zebulun? And I will draw unto thee to the river Kishon Sisera, the captain of Jabin's army, with his chariots and his multitude; and I will deliver him into thine hand.** And Barak said unto her, If thou wilt go with me, then I will go: but if thou wilt not go with me, then I will not go. And she said, I will surely go with thee: **notwithstanding the journey that thou takest shall not be for thine honour; for the Lord shall sell Sisera into the hand of a woman.** And Deborah arose, and went with Barak to Kedesh.*

JUDGES 4:6-9

After twenty years of oppression the people finally began praying and calling upon the Lord and Deborah released the prophetic word. Two things were at play here:

❖ The people prayed.

❖ The prophetic was released:

And Sisera gathered together all his chariots, even nine hundred chariots of iron, and all the people that were with him, from Harosheth of the Gentiles unto the river of Kishon. And Deborah said unto Barak, Up; for this is the day in which the Lord hath delivered Sisera into thine hand: is not the Lord gone out before thee? So Barak went down from mount Tabor, and ten thousand men after him. And the Lord discomfited Sisera, and all his chariots, and all his host, with the edge of the sword before Barak; so that Sisera lighted down off his chariot, and fled away on his feet. But Barak pursued after the chariots, and after the host, unto Harosheth of the Gentiles: and all the host of Sisera fell upon the edge of the sword; and there was not a man left. Howbeit Sisera fled away on his feet to the tent of Jael the wife of Heber the Kenite: for there was peace between Jabin the king of Hazor and the house of Heber the Kenite. And Jael went out to meet Sisera, and said unto him, Turn in, my lord, turn in to me; fear not. And when he had turned in unto her into the tent, she covered him with a mantle. And he said unto her, Give me, I pray thee, a little water to drink; for I am thirsty. And she opened a bottle of milk, and gave him drink, and covered him. Again he said unto her, Stand in the door of the tent, and it shall be, when any man doth come and enquire of thee, and say, Is there any man here? that thou shalt say, No. Then Jael Heber's wife took a nail of the tent, and took an hammer in her hand, and went softly unto him, and smote the nail into his temples, and fastened it into the ground: for he was fast asleep and weary. So he died.

JUDGES 4:13-21

In the natural it looked an impossibility for Sisera to lose but something strange happened. The Message Translation writes: '*God routed Sisera— all those chariots, all those troops!—before Barak. Sisera jumped out of his chariot and ran. Barak chased the chariots and troops all the way to Harosheth Haggoyim. Sisera's entire fighting force was killed—not one man left.*' The end result was that Sisera fled and went to the house of Heber. Being so tired, he slept and Jael, Heber's wife drove a nail in his head and he died at the hand of a woman – as the prophecy revealed. How was it possible for Israel – who had been pinned down for twenty years – to overcome the great general, Sisera? Deborah reveals what was going on in the spirit world:

They fought from heaven; the stars in their courses fought against Sisera. The river of Kishon swept them away, that ancient river, the river Kishon. O my soul, thou hast trodden down strength. Then were the horsehoofs broken by the means of the pransings, the pransings of their mighty ones.

JUDGES 5:20-22

Sisera looked invincible in the natural but he lost the battle in the spiritual. See what the John Gills' Exposition of the Bible Commentary says:

They fought from heaven... Either the angels of heaven, afterwards called stars; or the heavens, the elements, fought for Israel, and against Sisera; a violent storm of rain and hail falling at this time, which discomfited Sisera's army; See Gill on Judges 4:15, or this victory was obtained in such a manner as plainly showed it was not of man, but of God from heaven; so the Targum,"from heaven war was made with them;"with the kings before mentioned; God fought against them, and no wonder they were conquered:

The stars in their courses fought against Sisera it seems as if it was in the night that this battle was fought, at least that the pursuit lasted till night, when the stars by their brightness and clear shining favoured the Israelites, and were greatly to the disadvantage of the

Canaanites; unless it can be thought, as is by some, that the stars had an influence to cause a tempest of rain, hail, thunder, and lightnings, by which the army of Sisera was discomfited in the daytime, as before observed.

Josephus, the historian reported that just as the battle began, a violent storm broke out, with a great downpour of rain. God sent rain, torrential rain, as the heavens dropped. The River Kishon's banks overflowed and the mudslides from the mountain came down, creating a perfect storm. The war chariots and the horses got bogged down. Having sunk in the mud, the wheels with the scythes no longer turned, causing the soldiers to abandon their positions and jump off, only to be stuck in the mud and killed by Barak's men. Sisera thought he escaped, only to be nailed in the head by Jael.

All this points to the battle *being won in the heavenlies* to create a better present and future. Sisera's invincibility was broken because the *stars* fought against him; in the Scriptures, angels are often referred to as stars:

The mystery of the seven stars which thou sawest in my right hand, and the seven golden candlesticks. The seven stars are the angels of the seven churches: and the seven candlesticks which thou sawest are the seven churches.

REVELATION 1:20

When the morning stars sang together, and all the sons of God shouted for joy?

JOB 8:37

As Israel cried unto the Lord in prayer and the prophetic word was released, there was a war in the unseen realm. The demons and the principality which had helped Sisera to dominate Israel for twenty years were overcome as Israel cried unto the Lord. Twenty years of oppression came to an end as a shift happened in the spirit. The change in the spirit resulted in a perfect storm that allowed Israel to obtain the victory over Sisera. I submit to you that as you maintain the prayer pressure on your prophetic destiny, there will be a divine shift to create a better present and future for you.

6 SPIRITUAL WARFARE IS BREAKING THE RESISTANCE OF OPPOSING SPIRITUAL FORCES

Daniel epitomized this reality. We can glean a lot from the conversation between the angel and Daniel:

> *Then said he unto me, Fear not, Daniel: for from the first day that thou didst set thine heart to understand, and to chasten thyself before thy God, thy words were heard, and I am come for thy words. But the prince of the kingdom of Persia withstood me one and twenty days: but, lo, Michael, one of the chief princes, came to help me; and I remained there with the kings of Persia.*
>
> DANIEL 10:12-13

You need to grasp that:

❖ Daniel prayed, God answered but a demonic principality hindered.

❖ Earth called, heaven answered but the spirit realm resisted.

❖ Daniel persisted in prayer and fasting and broke the opposing spiritual force.

Your unbending and unrelenting attitude in prayer will cause the enemy to back down. I am not talking about psyching yourself up but maintaining the prayer pressure. Something has to yield and break. It is not going to be God for He is the same yesterday today and forever. When the devil finds out that you will not yield and break, you will have resisted him and he will flee from you. Remember, Jesus told a parable with the view that man ought always to pray and not to faint.

Now connect that with what we are told in Proverbs:

If thou faint in the day of adversity, thy strength is small.

PROVERBS 24:10

Fainting and prayerlessness go together. God has so clearly told us to put up spiritual resistance: '*Resist the devil, and he will flee from you*' (James 4:7). Let's look at some more verses to establish this fact:

And the seventy returned again with joy, saying, Lord, even the devils are subject unto us through thy name. And he said unto them, I beheld Satan as lightning fall from heaven. Behold, I give unto you power to tread on serpents and scorpions, and over all the power of the enemy: and nothing shall by any means hurt you.

LUKE 10:17-19

Fight the good fight of faith, lay hold on eternal life, whereunto thou art also called, and hast professed a good profession before many witnesses.

1 TIMOTHY 6:12

Be sober, be vigilant; because your adversary the devil, as a roaring lion, walketh about, seeking whom he may devour: Whom resist stedfast in the faith, knowing that the same afflictions are accomplished in your brethren that are in the world.

1 PETER 5:8-9

Through thee will we push down our enemies: through thy name will we tread them under that rise up against us.

PSALM 44:5

For thou hast girded me with strength unto the battle: thou hast subdued under me those that rose up against me. Thou hast also given me the necks of mine enemies; that I might destroy them that hate me.

PSALM 18:39-40

*And it came to pass, when they brought out those kings unto Joshua,
that Joshua called for all the men of Israel, and said unto the captains
of the men of war which went with him, Come near, put your feet upon
the necks of these kings. And they came near, and put their feet upon the
necks of them. And Joshua said unto them, Fear not, nor be dismayed,
be strong and of good courage: for thus shall the Lord do to all your
enemies against whom ye fight.*

JOSHUA 10:24-25

Even as Joshua called for all the men of Israel, our Heavenly Joshua, the
Lord Jesus Christ has called us to put our feet upon the necks of our enemies.
This is God's promise to those who will fight, *'for thus shall the Lord do to
all your enemies against whom ye fight.'*

7 SPIRITUAL WARFARE TAKES YOU AWAY FROM BEING A PREY TO BECOMING A PREDATOR

Finally, as we come to the end of this book, understand spiritual warfare
makes you a predator and not a prey. When you pray like Jesus, you will
never be a prey for the enemy. The devil preys upon people who do not pray.
One of my favorite verses in the Bible is found in Psalms:

*Blessed be the Lord, who hath not given us as a prey to their teeth. Our
soul is escaped as a bird out of the snare of the fowlers: the snare is
broken, and we are escaped.*

PSALM 124:6-7

If the Lord has not given you as prey to your enemy's teeth then it means
you will not be devoured. Peter also had something to say about this:

*Be sober, be vigilant; because your adversary the devil, as a roaring lion,
walketh about, seeking whom he may devour: Whom resist stedfast in
the faith, knowing that the same afflictions are accomplished in your
brethren that are in the world.*

1 PETER 5:8-9

Yes the devil roams around like a roaring lion, seeking whom he may devour. It did not say he devours everybody and anybody; he is looking for easy prey that will not resist him. Peter admonished us: *'whom resist steadfast in the faith...'* The choice is clearly ours! Paul put it this way:

Neither give place to the devil.

EPHESIANS 4:27

We have to make the decision not to give any place to the devil. Don't see yourself as a victim who is subject to the whims of the devil. No! You are the redeemed of the Lord. You have His Word, His name, His armor, His Spirit and you are covered with His precious blood. You are not the prey here, you are the predator. Jesus told you: *'And these signs shall follow them that believe; In my name shall they cast out devils...'* (Mark 16:17). Now when you read that you may have an image of a preacher casting out a devil in someone who may be possessed or oppressed. This verse, however is for the believer: YOU are the believer who is to cast out devils.

You may ask, *'Are you saying I need to go and have deliverance services?'* No that is not what I am saying! This verse is telling us the first priority of the believer is to cast out devils. We do that by not giving him place in our homes, our families, our finances or our bodies. So instead of thinking of an exorcism, think about kicking the devil out of your house! If he is attacking your body then he is trespassing: Kick him out! God would not tell you to do something that He Himself did not and would not do:

And there was war in heaven: Michael and his angels fought against the dragon; and the dragon fought and his angels, And prevailed not; neither was their place found any more in heaven. And the great dragon was cast out, that old serpent, called the Devil, and Satan, which deceiveth the whole world: he was cast out into the earth, and his angels were cast out with him.

REVELATION 12:7-9

John the Revelator reveals that Satan and his cohorts fought against Michael and his angels but they were too weak to win therefore there was no place found for the devil and he was cast out. Let there be no place found in your home for the enemy. Let this be said about your house:

My house shall be called the house of prayer

MATTHEW 21:13

And let thy house be like the house of Pharez,

RUTH 4:12

Pharez means 'breakthrough'. When your house becomes the house of prayer it will become the home of breakthroughs. I want to challenge you to take up every prophetic declaration that has been uttered over your life and begin to do warfare with them. You must see the fulfillment of these words. Whatever you see in the Scripture that does not match your life then it is time to wield prayer as a weapon in spiritual warfare for fulfillment of prophetic future. It is time for you to contend in spiritual warfare for your destiny and the destinies of your children. You are the priest of your home; open your mouth wide and God will fill it. If you are not going to do it then who will? This is your time and your season. It is my prayer that as we have looked extensively at the prayer life of Jesus and the different dimensions of prayer that you would develop your prayer life accordingly.

Pray so that you will not be a prey!

ABOUT THE AUTHOR

D R. Glenn Arekion is a uniquely gifted teacher and conference speaker. He conveys the Word of Truth in a simple, yet dynamic and motivational, way. With more than two decades' experience, he travels the globe mentoring leaders, equipping businessmen, and ministering to people, helping them to fulfill their purpose in life. He is a captivating and much sought-after speaker.

The author of more than thirty books, Glenn is dedicated to transforming lives from defeat into victory. His teaching materials are sold in many countries and are popular among those with a desire to grow strong in faith and experience great success.

Glenn is apostolic in his thrust of ministry. He believes in teaching and training pastors in their calling. His television program, *Faithlift*, airs twice a week on The Word Network. *Faithlift* is also a weekly television program on a number of networks that broadcast across the US, Africa, the U.K. and all over Europe.

Born in Mauritius, but raised and educated in London, Glenn holds a master's degrees and three doctorate degrees.

Glenn and his beautiful wife, Rosanna, have three children – Lisa, Ethan, and Jodie – and reside in Kentucky.

Author Contact

Glenn Arekion Ministries
P.O. Box 197777
Louisville, KY 40259, USA
mail@glennarekion.org
www.glennarekion.org

Further books by Dr Glenn Arekion...

Available online at glennarekion.org
Download eBooks and MP3 messages instantly

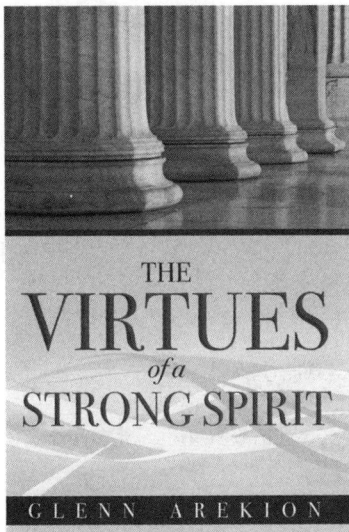

THE
VIRTUES
of a
STRONG SPIRIT

GLENN AREKION

God created man with words of dominion and His original intent was for man to live from the inside out. This simply means to dominate the flesh from the spirit, and the natural from the spiritual. Since the fall of Adam, man has been living from his flesh, dominated by circumstances. Through the regeneration, our spirit man was reborn to win but the key is to know how to have a strong spirit. The stronger we are in our spirit the easier it will be for us to resist the attacks of the devil.

Living in the last days, it is imperative for the believer to be strong in spirit, to overcome the relentless attacks of the world, the flesh and the devil. Paul, the apostle, commanded the Ephesian believers to be 'Strong in the Lord'. How does one do that? He is not talking about our physical muscles. It is in the working out of our spirit man that we can truly be strong.

This book will unveil the secrets of spiritual strength and the consequences of having a weak spirit, such as:

- The stronger you are in your spirit, the more miracles and breakthroughs you will experience.
- The stronger you are in your spirit, the easier it will be for you to resist the attacks of the devil.
- The stronger you are in your spirit, the healthier you will be in your body.
- The stronger you are in your spirit, the less influence the world will have over you.

Further books by Dr Glenn Arekion...

Available online at glennarekion.org
Download eBooks and MP3 messages instantly

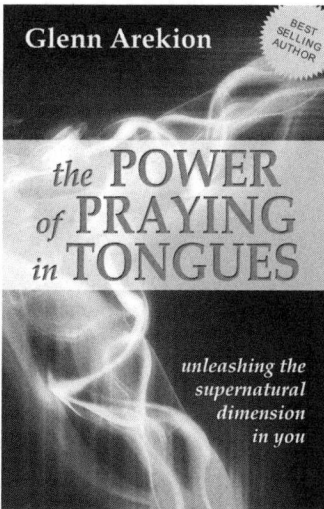

Glenn Arekion

BEST SELLING AUTHOR

the **POWER** of **PRAYING** in **TONGUES**

unleashing the supernatural dimension in you

Are you ready for the supernatural?

Tired of mundane, dead Christianity and want to see Bible days in your life? Then this book is for you!

"I thank my God, I speak with tongues more than ye all" (1 Corinthians 14:18). Paul, the greatest apostle who ever lived, who wrote close to two-thirds of the New Testament and gave you your foundations for living an effective Christian life, uttered these words.
This founding father of the faith deemed "praying in tongues" of utmost importance and was grateful that he partook of such a great blessing.

Prayer is a command and calling of God. The Lord Jesus Christ specifically mentioned that His house is to be the house of prayer.
If you are born again, then you form part of the family of God, and prayer is your calling.

In The Power of Praying in Tongues, you will learn:

- The importance of praying in tongues
- Sixty expository benefits of praying in tongues
- The roots of negativism concerning tongues
- To develop partnership with the Holy Spirit
- To tap into supernatural Christianity

Also available in French and Spanish.

Further books by Dr Glenn Arekion...

Available online at glennarekion.org
Download eBooks and MP3 messages instantly

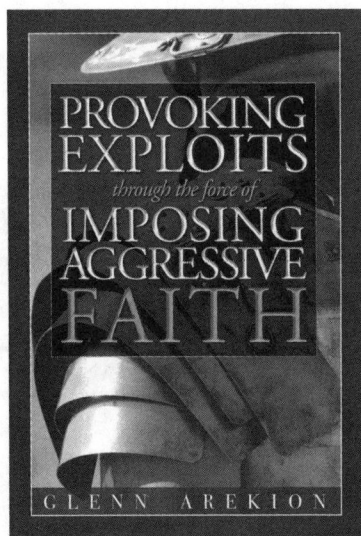

And such as do wickedly against the covenant shall he corrupt by flatteries: but the people that do know their God shall be strong, and do exploits - Daniel 11:32

The strength of your enemy is your ignorance. Those who are weak and ignorant will be exploited but those who are strong will have exploits. An exploit is a great feat that brings joy and every believer is called to a life of unlimited exploits - yet not every believer is experiencing this quality of life. Why? There are some key life-elements and attributes that are likely missing. Using Daniel 11:32 as the foundational verse, you will learn the prophecy and the history that this verse refers to. From the text, Glenn unravels five key attributes the believer must have in order to lead a life of exploits, specifically:

- Knowing God
- Being strong
- Having Imposing, aggressive faith
- Persistent and importunate prayer
- The leading of the Spirit

For many believers, the time span between exploits is too long. The Scripture says, *'Blessed be the Lord, who daily loadeth us with benefits...'* (Psalm 68:19).

Therefore we can have daily exploits. Many books have been written about faith but this book will open up another vista that will boost your faith for supernatural exploits. These five attributes - when implemented in your life - will set you up for exploits. No longer will you be exploited!

Further books by Dr Glenn Arekion...

Available online at glennarekion.org
Download eBooks and MP3 messages instantly

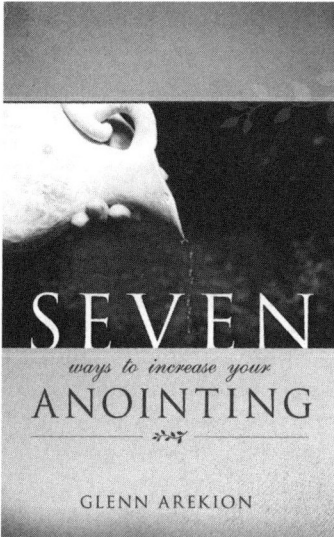

What you are about to read will revolutionize your life and take you to a higher dimension! The anointing is the most indispensable force in the life of the believer. With it, you will have the power and faith to do great exploits. Without it, life and ministry will be a constant source of frustration and irritation. Many have visions but simply do not know how to make the realities in their lives.

This book is full of answers to your most frustrating questions. The name of the game is results, and when you know how to purposely tap into the anointing and treasure of God, you will:

- Be transformed into a different person
- Be elevated into a new place in God
- Be the catalyst for positive change in the lives of suffering people
- See your dream become your destiny

Seven ways to increase your anointing will answer your heart's cry. It will show you how to remove the powerlessness and lack of influence in your life, while empowering you to do the mighty works of God.

Also available in French.

Further books by Dr Glenn Arekion...

Available online at glennarekion.org
Download eBooks and MP3 messages instantly

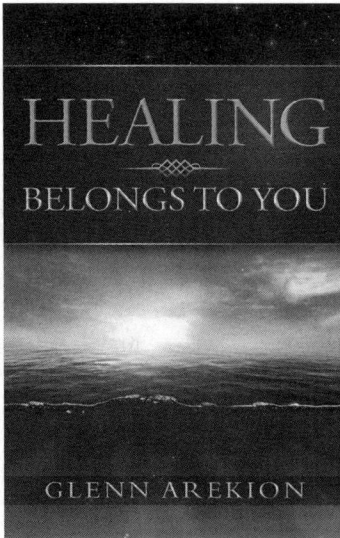

Jesus declared that healing is the children's bread. It is the divine right of every believer to walk in divine healing, divine health and divine life. However, as long as there are questions in your mind as to whether or not it is God's will to heal, your faith will be hampered from receiving what Jesus legally purchased for you.

Since Jesus Christ is the same yesterday, today and forever, He is still anointed to heal. The ministry of Jesus, today, is still a miraculous, healing ministry - as it was when he first walked the streets of Jerusalem and the shores of Galilee.

This book will answer the important healing questions and reveal God's thoughts towards your wellness. This book will eliminate doubts, banish fear and boost your faith to receive your inheritance. As you meditate upon the truths in these chapters, you will discover:

- Did healing pass away with the apostles?
- Is God glorified through sickness?
- Am I entitled to divine health in old age?
- How to resist sickness
- How to receive your healing
- 101 healing promises
- Daily healing confessions to cover your life

His Word is medicine to our flesh. He sent His Word and His Word healed them all. You are part of the "all" He sent his Word to heal. Receive your healing NOW!

Further books by Dr Glenn Arekion...

Available online at glennarekion.org
Download eBooks and MP3 messages instantly

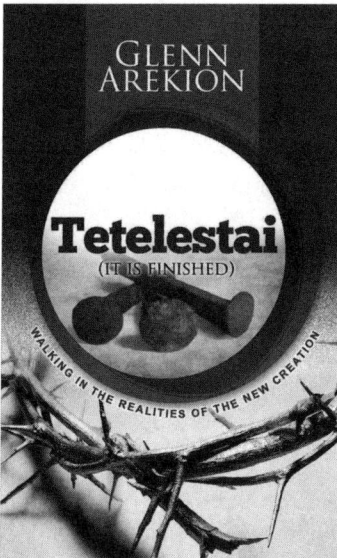

The apostle Paul had an understanding of the new creation like no other authors of the New Testament. What was passed on in the first Adam is now passed away in the last Adam! A revelation of the new creation in Christ will revolutionize your life. New-creation realities will enable you to dominate the old creation, that is the old man. In this powerful book, Dr Glenn Arekion unveils the power of the new man over the old man and the mindset of Paul by the explanation of:

- The finished work of Christ
- The curse of the law
- The blessing of Abraham
- The believer's position
- The realities of the new creation

Break free from the fallen genetics of the first Adam passed down to the human race and live from your new identity in Christ. This book will enlighten your understanding to your position in Jesus Christ. No longer will you accept the lies of the devil as the norms in your life.

Enjoy your new status in Christ over all the works of the enemy and walk in victory.

Also available in French.

Further books by Dr Glenn Arekion...

Available online at glennarekion.org
Download eBooks and MP3 messages instantly

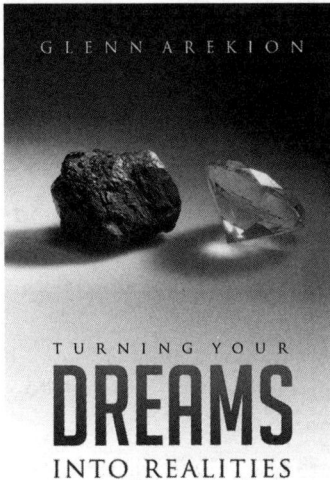

GLENN AREKION

TURNING YOUR

DREAMS

INTO REALITIES

'I'm living the dream' is an expression that is often said but hardly ever experienced. Much has been said in the past years about the importance of dreams and visions for a fulfilled life and yet there are more dissatisfied people today than ever. This is because without wisdom, strategies and disciplines, visions remain grounded. Many have not reached the lofty positions that their dreams had for them due to a lack of these three fundamental forces.

Solomon, the most successful entrepreneurial king, knew the keys to success and he said in Ecclesiastes, 'For a dream cometh through the multitude of business...' Modern translations render this verse as, 'A dream comes through by much business, much activities and painful efforts.' Sitting down and merely having a dream without activities, strategies and certain disciplines implemented in your life will not trigger your dream to materialize.

This book explains the necessary wisdom strategies and the corresponding disciplines that you need to turn your dreams into realities. In this book you will learn:

- You are the number one enterprise that you need to build
- To destroy the excuses people use to abort their destiny
- The values of goals and diversities of goals
- Time management
- The ten characteristics of the diligent
- The million dollar habits you need to develop
- Wisdom secrets from the ants, the conies, the locusts and the spiders
- To turn your dreams into realities

Further books by Dr Glenn Arekion...

Available online at glennarekion.org
Download eBooks and MP3 messages instantly

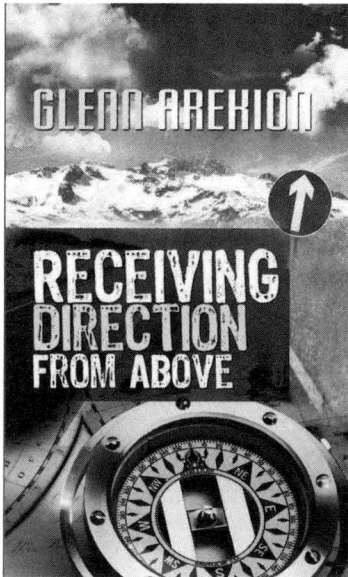

Whatever is troubling you is not troubling God. Whatever is disturbing you is certainly not disturbing God. Why? Because God knows what to do about your problem. The reason you are perturbed and troubled is due to the fact that you do not know what God knows. If you knew what he knew then you would be just like God: cool, calm and collected.

Having access to the voice of God is the right of every believer. He wants to speak to you.

In this powerful book, you will discover the secret of receiving direction from above. You will learn:

- How God speaks
- Why 'fleece' is not for the New Testament believer
- How God led the apostle Paul
- How to fine-tune your spirit man to pick up on the voice of God

This powerful book will change your life.

Further books by Dr Glenn Arekion...

Available online at glennarekion.org
Download eBooks and MP3 messages instantly

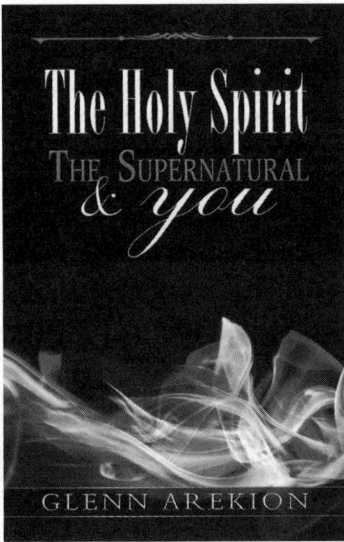

You are only as effective as the quality of the information you receive. As a believer, you will be empowered, enlightened and energized as the exciting truths become alive in your heart and mind.

This book is a toolbox for the believer and minister, equipping them to fix life's problems. Life and ministry without the Holy Spirit, the Supernatural and His gifts will be a cycle of frustration but with Him actively involved, Bible results will become your reality!

If you are tired of living your Christian life without results then you need this great tool in your hands TODAY.

Through this book, Dr Glenn helps you:

- To develop your relationship with the greatest partner – The Holy Spirit
- To attract an active partnership with the Holy Spirit
- To grasp the purpose and validity of the gifts of the Spirit
- How to activate the gifts in your life and ministry
- To know what Paul meant by 'the best gift'
- To understand what the supernatural means
- To release the supernatural in your life and ministry
- To delve into 101 benefits of praying Tongues
- To understand the efficacy of fasting for a supernatural ministry
- To keep the fire of God burning in your life

This book contains 13 powerful chapters that will help you in your walk with God.

Also available in French and Spanish.

Further books by Dr Glenn Arekion...

Available online at glennarekion.org
Download eBooks and MP3 messages instantly

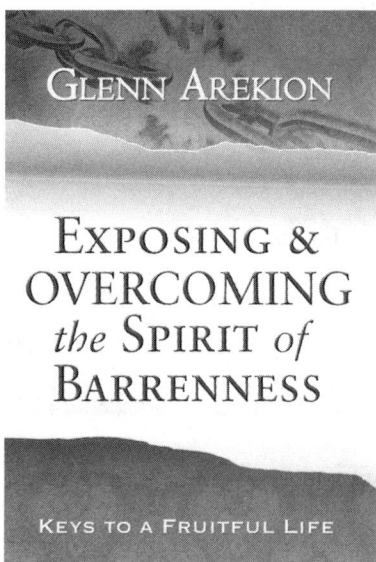

GLENN AREKION

EXPOSING & OVERCOMING *the* **SPIRIT** *of* **BARRENNESS**

KEYS TO A FRUITFUL LIFE

The first prophetic words ever spoken to humanity by Elohim were, "Be fruitful and multiply". Barrenness therefore is a direct assault, confrontation, violation and challenge to God's first decree to mankind. In this book you will discover that barrenness is not only a biological or a female problem and it operates on many different levels with different facets.

Barrenness is manifested:

- Biologically
- Territorially
- Financially
- Ministerially
- Generationally
- Mentally
- Professionally
- Spiritually
- Personally

When dealing with the spirit of barrenness, you are dealing with the spirit of stagnation and limitation. It seeks to curtail your life, your status, your ministry, your church, your family and your finances.

BUT IT CAN BE BROKEN!

In this book, Dr. Glenn gives you five powerful keys to destroy the spirit of barrenness and forbid it from ever operating in your life.

Further books by Dr Glenn Arekion...

Available online at glennarekion.org
Download eBooks and MP3 messages instantly

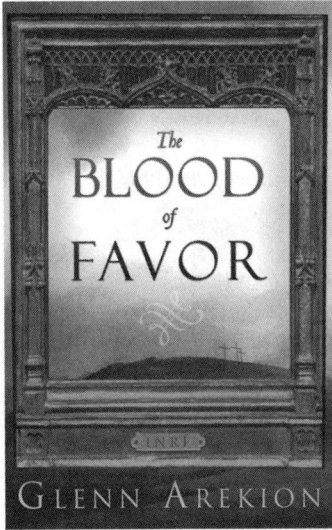

Does the sight of blood scare you? Make you shudder? Cause you to feel faint?

A childhood experience left Dr Glenn feeling this way for years – until he focused on the "precious blood of Christ" that provides eternal life and love.

Throughout time, the world has searched for the keys of protection and redemption. Every type of ritual, performance, and self-abasement imaginable has been attempted in this search while the true key has been overlooked.

The much neglected and noticeably overlooked subject of the blood of Christ trickling down the cross, which held captive His out-of-joint but unbroken body, is the answer that all of mankind has been waiting for. There are inexhaustible benefits of this uncommon blood; but before we can ever experience these benefits, we must first not only acknowledge them but also explore their possibilities.

This blood holds within it manifold blessings because of the covenant which it represents, whether it is approached for the salvation of a loved one, forgiveness of sin, or when the storms of life come upon us. This book will show you a step-by-step process to the victory in life that the precious blood of Christ holds. May Heaven kiss you and grant you its favor as you dig deeply into these anointed words.

People Like You... Make People Like Me... Go!

So two good things happen as a result of your gifts—those in need are helped, and they overflow with thanks to God. Those you help will be glad not only because of your generous gifts to themselves and others, but they will praise God for this proof that your deeds are as good as your doctrine. And they will pray for you with deep fervor and feeling because of the wonderful grace of God shown through you

2 Corinthians 9:12-14 – Living Bible

Every major ministry making an impact in the world today is blessed with faithful financial and prayerful partners. Partnership with a ministry is a crucial way for the Gospel to go in all the world. Together, I am totally convinced that we can impact the world and accomplish great things to the glory of God.

I have a simple vision burning in my spirit and that is to unveil the Good News to sinners and saints that victory is available in life through Jesus Christ. Therefore partners are an important part of this ministry and their assistance enable us to accomplish the following:

❖ Globally preach the Gospel through the media: The Word Network;
❖ Travel and preach the Gospel to the nations;
❖ Author books anointed by the Holy Spirit, endowed with information that will radically transform the lives of believers;
❖ Healing crusades and conventions worldwide;
❖ Planting churches in different nations.

Partners help us to do what we cannot do by ourselves.

Not everyone is called to full time ministry but every one is called to reach our world. Everyone who actively participates in supporting Glenn Arekion Ministries with their finances and prayers will receive credit and rewards for whatever this ministry accomplishes.

So join me as a partner today and be part of this end-time harvest! Together, let's reach the millions who need to hear the gospel of Jesus Christ. Your partnership with me will give you the personal satisfaction of being part of a strong ministry that is doing its best to fulfill the Great Commission. You can have the confidence of sowing into a ministry of integrity, knowing that your support is accomplishing the work of the gospel.

Visit **glennarekion.org/partner** today and join us!